THIRTY-THREE
BREATHS

A LITTLE BOOK ON MEDITATION

REV. JOHN J. LOMBARDI

CATHEDRAL
FOUNDATION PRESS

Imprimatur
✠ William E. Lori
Archbishop of Baltimore
March 30, 2017

This *imprimatur* is given with the understanding that it indicates that there is nothing within the work that is contrary to the faith and morals of the Roman Catholic Church as it is proposed by the ecclesiastical magisterium. This *imprimatur* does not imply any agreement with the author's theories or hypotheses within the work, nor to the truthfulness of any citations or other sources. All work is solely that of the author.

PUBLISHED BY

CATHEDRAL
FOUNDATION PRESS
© 2017, FATHER JOHN J. LOMBARDI

Printed and bound in the United States of America
2 3 4 5
Library of Congress Catalog Card Number 2017046385
ISBN 978-1-885938-52-7

PUBLISHED BY: Cathedral Foundation Press
PUBLISHER: Christopher Gunty
COVER AND BOOK DESIGN: Sara Travlos
COVER PHOTO BY: Vince Protani
COVER PHOTO: Kenai Peninsula
PRINTED IN THE USA

"Through the study of books one seeks God; by meditation one finds him."

– St. Padre Pio

IN MEMORY OF

my Mom, *Rose Ann*:
A Mystical Rose-gift to me,
Who passed this year:
Thank you, Love you, See you!...

And to

Dad: who loved her faithfully,
and gifted this Book-adventure
bountifully!

THANK YOU TO ALL my donors, supporters in this venture who gave graciously—financially, materially, spiritually!

Special thanks to staff members and parishioners of St. Peter and St. Patrick Churches, including Amanda Miller, Sandra Meijer and Judy Dudich.

And thanks to Woodeene Koenig-Bricker, who helped immensely with organizing and editing the manuscript.

CONTENTS

INTRODUCTION

"Meditation is, above all, a quest.
The mind seeks to understand...
and respond to what the Lord is asking."

– CATECHISM OF THE CATHOLIC CHURCH #2705

Today, everyone's stressed.
Or doing yoga.
Which one are you into?
Or trying to get away from?

"BE LIKE MIKE..."

ALLOW ME TO TELL YOU A STORY
ABOUT PRAYER AND MEDITATION.

After pulling a muscle and suffering from lower back pain for a couple of months, a friend gave me a ride to the doctor. We went into a frenzied waiting room, a busy, bustling office with three TVs mounted on walls, simultaneously blaring three different channels. One TV showcased a noxious talk show. Another was a 24-hour news station and the third was a cooking show. Patients were constantly coming in and out and a grumbling client and staff member at the admissions window were having an argument. (Some folks looked at me in my Roman collar as if imploring me to do something.) Cell phones were ringing, nurses were calling for patients, the bathroom fan was running, and doors were noisily opening and shutting. Not a healing or peaceful place, right?

As I sat down to fill out my registration form, I was wondering how long I would be able to tolerate all this going on. I looked over at my friend, Mike, expecting him to be fuming with a red face or shouting to get out of this toxic atmosphere. Instead, he looked like the sculpture by Rodin, "The Thinker"—casual and meditative. He appeared as a relaxed, "secular monk." As I watched him, I saw he was praying, holding a prayer book in his lap. His eyes were closed, his legs were crossed, and his head tilted down in spiritual poise and pose, all while sitting directly underneath one of the darned blaring TVs! He put me to shame. I, the priest, was totally distracted; yet, it seemed as though, to him, nothing else existed other than his peaceful communion with God.

That's a great image of prayer, or, more specifically, meditation. Everyone can pray, but not everyone can meditate in a waiting room in the midst of a stressful situation. Not everyone is a "pro" like Mike who can enter into deeper prayer against all those odds. So, to become a "pro"—or just accomplished—we must work at meditation like anything else at which we hope to succeed. We must strive to "be like Mike."

Mike learned from past Church history and, in specific, St. Josemaria Escrivá (a Spanish saint who founded a religious order, Opus Dei, with an emphasis to form lay people in deeper spirituality). In essence, the saint encourages, "Pray where you are"—don't cave in just because you're busy or are in a frantic waiting room or you can't get into a church. Enough of the excuses! That day when I looked over at Mike, as the TV blared and the toxicity enveloped us, he was transfixed in his prayer book—just a few feet from the chaos as though it wasn't even there. That's when I made up my mind to "be like Mike."

Did you know that Christians "owe it to themselves to develop the desire to meditate regularly"? (Catechism of the Catholic Church, #2707, hereafter CCC) That's what the Catholic Church (and others) calls each and all of us to do!

Simply put, this *Little Book* is more "how-to" meditate than words explaining meditation. It emphasizes the "nuts, bolts, and guts"— meditative pragmatism, rather than theological theory. The essence of this book can be summarized by the following advertisement I saw years ago in a news magazine. I can't remember the product advertised, but the caption read, "Don't just do something. Sit there."

You got it. That bold, iconoclastic advertisement upends the ordinary way of thinking and doing. Everyone's busy these days—or they say they are—stressed out, over-committed, multi-tasking. The advertisement suspends your knee-jerk "do-it-ism" and calls you to stop it all. That's what meditation does and is: sitting in God's Presence and focusing on his ways.

All types of books are available on mindfulness, meditation, and a plethora of types of spirituality one can choose (since no one is into "religion" anymore—more on that later). In our land of infinite re-invention, we see many promotions and promises for "New Life"—such as the book *10 Percent Happier* by Dan Harris, which states meditation will do just that for you—make you ten percent happier. Then there's the Dalai Lama, traveling all over the world and attracting by his mystic dimension and offering age-old spirituality from the East. There's also Joseph Goldstein of Buddhist meditation circles offering calming meditation techniques and endless Hindu yogis or gurus, East and West, spreading a kind of "Gospel of Mindfulness."

But, what about Catholics and non-Catholic Christians? Basically, we've "got it" but must "get it out there"! That means "marketing" prayerful Christian spirituality and meditation in worldly yet wise ways, and more assertively—after all, spirituality is our strong suit, not just the clichéd bingo games and fish frys.

Let's always remember, despite what you think of "religious folks" or Catholics or non-Catholic Christians, it is our Leader, our Master, Jesus Christ, who instructs us to follow a meditative life, as in: "Come away by yourselves, to a deserted place and rest a while" (Mk. 6:31). Saints and meditation masters have used this biblical text to form a life of stillness and silence, an "interior life." This *Little Book* follows these and other words of Our Lord.

So, simply remember, as this *Little Book* tells you often: sit in silence and stillness, in your car, on lunch break, while waiting for the kids, during a walk or hike, and "wait on the Lord" and pray in peace, allowing him to pacify your mind and heart. Simply say his name, "Jesus," or "Lord" or "Most High," or one of my favorite short prayers: "Lord Jesus I need you, I love you, I trust you." Repeat slowly within, perhaps imaging his glory, and thus be able to receive his graces. This is a form of meditation, interior prayer.

> "Spiritual progress tends toward ever more intimate union with Christ. This union is called 'mystical' because it participates in the mystery of Christ through the sacraments —'the holy mysteries'—and, in him, in the mystery of the Holy Trinity. God calls us all to this intimate union with him, even if the special graces or extraordinary signs of this mystical life are granted only to some for the sake of manifesting the gratuitous gift given to all" (CCC 2014).

Just what is meditation? As we shall find out later in this *Little Book*, it essentially consists of the elements C-I-A. Meditation is a sustained action of *Concentration*. You have to settle down, chill!

Second it is *Internal* rather than external activity. Our minds are powerful-transformational engines and storehouses of activity! Lastly, meditation is *Affective:* it's not just heady stuff but loving God and his holy ways with emotions and sentiments—a way to "glue" or affectively affix our souls to Him.

There are many ways to meditate, but they all involve the above attributes. Whether it's using a religious picture or icon for inspiration, a sacred word (or aspiration or mantra), or Bible verse, meditation is paradoxically simple and difficult. Simple in that there are not many steps or things to do, and yet challenging because we are so used to external stimulations and we might easily get distracted or jittery by focusing or "going inside."

In the chapters ahead you will review the sacred writings and saints of "inner Christianity" who gave us the groundwork for meditation. We will learn how meditation is related to the general spiritual life and Christian prayer. And since this is a "how-to "book, we will present and learn some practice-exercises of meditation.

So, what is this *Little Book* about? In chapter one you'll learn a "Holy History." Chapter two covers "What is Meditation?" Chapter three is titled "Meditation and Prayer." We study "Aspects of Prayer and Meditation" in chapter four and "The Essence and Examples of Meditation" in chapter five.

A note on the title, *Thirty-Three Breaths*. Breathing is an obvious, physical, essential life process. Everyone must do it! Breathing 33 breaths, in a rhythmic and measured manner, is a way to both imitate Jesus' number of years of life on earth and also physically and spiritually pray in a simple and relatively short way. There's a lot there, but we'll get to all this breath-bliss later!

We are naturally born, they say, with a God-shaped hole within, and only God can fill it. In this *Little Book*, we will whet your appetite and offer one answers to filling that hole as the art and discipline of meditation. We are meant not only to find God but also to routinely connect with him through serene stillness and silence within the temples of our souls.

READ ON FOR MORE!

CHAPTER ONE

HOLY HISTORY

"RAPT IN MEDITATION, BEFORE THE HOLY EUCHARIST, UNBEKNOWNST TO ANYONE"...

N ow on to what I call "holy history." What have significant and celebrated persons throughout the ages taught us about prayer and meditation? St. Paul states in the Book of Galatians: "I live, no longer I, but Christ within me" (Gal. 2:20). Though we are mere humans, God dwells within us and meditation is the quest to reveal this indwelling.

St. Augustine, an early convert from paganism, wrote, "Late, have I loved you, O Beauty ever ancient ever true. ... You were within me, but I was without." While we do find God in the world, God is also within, as this saint discovered.

St. Athanasius said, "God became man that man might become God." This is the process known, especially in the East, as *theosis*, participating in godlikeness, which is accentuated by the practice of meditation and perhaps is the best-kept secret of Christianity.

St. Ignatius of Loyola and the Jesuit order he founded live by the motto "Contemplatives in action." This is the whole Gospel of Jesus and what we are to live through meditation practiced daily.

St. Mother Teresa of Kolkata said that we should encounter Christ through meditation in the Blessed Sacrament (Holy Eucharist) but also in the poor. This uniquely Christian biblical teaching is the true embodiment of Jesus' summation of the Mosaic Law—love God and love neighbor (Lk. 10:27).

St. John Paul II, while on his papal visit to Baltimore in October 1995, became "lost." He could not be located by the secret service or the resident bishop who hosted him. Later, he was found in a chapel, kneeling in rapt meditation before the Holy Eucharist—unbeknownst to anyone else.

These are just a few examples from the history of meditation in the Catholic and Christian tradition, but this is *A Little Book on Meditation*, not an encyclopedia, nor a "history book of spirituality" and so we are just going to hit some of the highlights in our brief overview of our spiritual past and how all that has affected meditation—and our own practice. In other words, we'll gain some history, inspiration, and guidance for meditation itself.

Now, first off, let's recall our "spiritual DNA." We are meant to commune and communicate with God, the Blessed Trinity, especially in an interior life, through meditation. Recall the story of when Jesus says to the Samaritan woman at the well, thirsting for something: "Everyone who drinks this water will be thirsty again; but whoever drinks the water I shall give will never thirst; the water I shall give will become in him a spring of water welling up to eternal life" (Jn. 4:13-14). We all have within us a supernatural potency for God and we have been given and need to practice dispositions and disciplines to commune with him. Meditation is one of those.

In our Christian heritage, we know our sacred religion and practices didn't just come from "out of the blue" but from Jewish and Eastern roots.

For instance, pious Jews would ruminate over the Torah and Pentateuch of Moses (first books of the Bible) and especially over the Psalms, and still do so today. This spiritual act of meditation is the opposite of reading the daily newspaper. Jews read their revered ancient scriptures and actually reflect on them, in deep consideration of their meaning within so they can fully imbibe the wisdom of God as He intended it for them.

A MEDITATION MOSAIC

THE BIBLE

The Bible is a book of and for prayer. There is a whole book in it of prayers (Psalms) and many prayers in the books. (The word Bible comes from the Greek, *biblos*, which means books; thus, essentially, the bible is a library compendium of God's teachings.)

As we mentioned previously, the Jewish practice of Torah meditation show the seedlings of meditative practice in our heritage. The Bible is holy because it sanctifies—makes sacred those who read and ponder it— "meditate on it day and night" (Ps. 1:2), as it is filled with many counsels on prayer-meditation.

OLD TESTAMENT

Prayer, classically defined, is speaking and listening to God; it is a conversation. In all times and through all occasions, we should converse with God, not only when we're in trouble but continuously! The first prayer in the Bible? Some say it is found in Genesis chapter 3, the conversation between Adam and Eve when they were hiding from the

Lord after sinning and the subsequent conversation between Adam and God, where Adam seeks to hide from God:

When they heard the sound of the Lord God walking about in the garden at the breezy time of the day, the man and his wife hid themselves from the Lord God among the trees of the garden. The Lord God then called to the man and asked him: "Where are you?" He answered, "I heard you in the garden; but I was afraid, because I was naked, so I hid." Then God asked: "Who told you that you were naked? Have you eaten from the tree of which I had forbidden you to eat?" The man replied, "The woman whom you put here with me—she gave me fruit from the tree, so I ate it." The Lord God then asked the woman: "What is this you have done?" The woman answered, "The snake tricked me, so I ate it."

Then the Lord God said to the snake: "Because you have done this, cursed are you among all the animals, tame or wild; On your belly you shall crawl, and dust you shall eat all the days of your life."

"I will put enmity between you and the woman, and between your offspring and hers; They will strike at your head, while you strike at their heel."

To the woman he said: "I will intensify your toil in childbearing; in pain you shall bring forth children. Yet your urge shall be for your husband, and he shall rule over you."

To the man he said: "Because you listened to your wife and ate from the tree about which I commanded you, You shall not eat from it, Cursed is the ground because of you! In toil you shall eat its yield all the days of your life. Thorns and thistles it shall bear for you, and you shall eat the grass of the field. By the sweat of your brow you shall eat bread.

4

Until you return to the ground, from which you were taken;
For you are dust, and to dust you shall return" (Gn. 3: 8–19).

Later, in Genesis 4:26, we read that creatures began "calling to the Lord"—after Adam and Eve conceived their children. Obviously a prayer! So then, call on God at all times.

In the Garden of Eden, before the Fall (original sin) Adam and Eve naturally "walked with God" and conversed with God, probably not as we do with formal prayer, but more informally because they were friends with God, not the sinners they became as after the Fall. Now, we, as sinners, "pray" (formally talk with God) because we want always to be in proper unity and harmony with God.

In Genesis 2:7, we read, "then the Lord God formed the man out of the dust of the ground and blew into his nostrils the breath of life, and the man became a living being." This passage shows the intimacy of God with humanity and the breathing aspect which we will later highlight later in our Book and practice.

In Exodus 3:14, we are told: "And God said, 'I Am Who Am.'" This emphasizes God's pure being, his sheer existence without any reliance upon an other. In meditation we can, as we settle more in silence and stillness, tap into the root of all being, God himself, kind of like plunging ourselves deep into the earth and grounding ourselves more solidly.

A few more passages from the Old Testament:

Joshua 1:8 describes how to observe the Law of God, to meditate upon it, for good success: "Do not let this book of the law depart from your lips. Recite it by day and by night, that you may carefully observe all that is written in it; then you will attain your goal; then you will succeed."

Jesus, as a good Jew, probably memorized the Psalms, which is useful for us as well. To meditate, we need these texts and if we have them memorized we can pray anywhere anytime!

- Psalm 1:2: Memorize this one!—"Rather the law of the Lord is his joy, and on his law he meditates day and night." Psalm

46:10. Especially for those times when you are enervated and don't believe in the necessity of slowing down, or to stop, always remember: "Be still and know that I am God."

- Psalm 19:15 reminds us: "Let the words of my mouth be acceptable, the thoughts of my heart before you, Lord, my rock and my redeemer."

- Psalm 119:15 tell us: "I will ponder your precepts and consider your paths."

THE SONG OF SONGS

Some wonder why this erotic-evocative book, which never mentions God (explicitly), should even be in the Bible. Famously (or infamously) it is one of the most copied and commented upon and prized books of the Middle Ages, as sages saw in it a love relationship between—take your pick—a man, a woman, as an illustration of God's love for Israel (as many Jews saw it) or, more universally, as an ecstatic duet between God and the soul.

SONGS 3:1
"On my bed at night I sought him
whom my soul loves...."

SONGS 4:7
"You are beautiful in every way, my friend..."

SONGS 5:4
"My lover put his hand in through the opening: my
innermost being trembled because of him."

NEW TESTAMENT

In the Book of Revelation we read Christ's offer to meet us: "Behold, I stand at the door and knock. If anyone hears my voice and opens the door, [then] I will enter his house and dine with him, and he with me" (Rev. 3:20). In essence, are you opening the door to your soul, going into that deep room within and encountering God—daily?

Here are some New Testament passages that encourage us to do just this:

- Luke 2:19—The Blessed Virgin Mary is said to have "kept all these things (God's revelations), reflecting on them in her heart."

- Mark 6:31—Christ himself invites us: "Come away by yourselves to a deserted place and rest a while."

- Luke 18:1-5—Jesus counsels the disciples on not getting weary in prayer with the somewhat comic-satiric example of a woman banging on a negligent-sleeping-weary judges' door:

   Then he (Jesus) told them a parable about the necessity for them to pray always without becoming weary. He said, "There was a judge in a certain town who neither feared God nor respected any human being. And a widow in that town used to come to him and say, 'Render a just decision for me against my adversary.' For a long time the judge was unwilling, but eventually he thought, 'While it is true that I neither fear God nor respect any human being, because this widow keeps bothering me I shall deliver a just decision for her lest she finally come and strike me.'"

- Matthew 6:5-6—Jesus warns us not to just babble or repeat old patterns of prayer but, rather, to be close to God within a "special place" and nurture an interior life:

   When you pray, do not be like the hypocrites, who love to stand and pray in the synagogues and on street corners so

7

that others may see them. Amen, I say to you, they have received their reward. But when you pray, go to your inner room, close the door, and pray to your Father in secret. And your Father who sees in secret will repay you.

- Matthew 26: 39-44—Contrary to being against repeating prayers, which He is not, Jesus himself in the Garden of Eden, prayed three times, "Father, if it is Your Will, let this cup pass me by…" showing us to ask, ask again and be steadfast in prayer (that goes for meditation and any kind of prayers and disciplines).

- I Thessalonians 5:17—"Pray without ceasing." Simply put, even though we take and make special times and places for meditation, sitting still, still we are called to pray unceasingly. This may mean many things (and probably does!), but we should always be praying, at least in our heart, with out desires. We should be praying everywhere. We should cultivate many forms of prayer, and we should live a life of prayer.

- 1 Timothy 4:15—"Be diligent in these matters, be absorbed in them, so that your progress may be evident to everyone." Our meditation should benefit everyone, not just ourselves. In other words, our meditation should make us better people in our dealings with others, so that they, too, are positively affected by our prayers.

SAYINGS OF THE SAINTS

Many saints from the early Church fathers such as Irenaeus, John Chrysostom and Athanasius to the present times stress divinization (or *deois, theosis*)—the healing-raising of our human nature's participation in God's nature by His grace and our purification of sin. This is summarized by the early Orthodox saying attributed to many and later to St. Thomas Aquinas: "God became a man that man might become God." We emphasize, and the Church Fathers did also, that we are not God by nature but are granted by God to participate in his nature by his grace, mercy and his free action. This "divinizing process" is effected by God, first by His grace and then through deeper prayer, contemplation and of course by an active way of life as a devout Christian.

Here is a sampling of the teaching of the saints.

THE EAST-HESYCHAST TRADITION (developed in Egypt, Syria, and Lebanon) emphasizes a rhythm of prayer, aligned with calm breathing, and sometimes in unison with praying the "Jesus prayer," which is: "Lord Jesus Christ, only Son of God, have mercy on me, a sinner." This ancient prayer, based upon the Bible, kept on the lips and in the heart is the subject of the spiritual classic, *The Way of a Pilgrim*, and is based on various Gospel narratives and short prayers and through heartfelt repetition, often occasioned with rosary beads.

ST. ANTHONY OF EGYPT (251-356) also known as St. Anthony of the Desert, was a progenitor of monasticism as he was originally a hermit and then formed a community and eventually passed on this way of life to many other followers, influenced them greatly, with the main elements emphasized being "watchfulness," purification of the heart, silence, humility, and stillness of mind and holy poverty, all virtues we should emulate.

DESERT FATHERS, who lived in third through fifth century were men who left downtown Cairo and the glitz of the pyramids, the hustle and bustle and intellectualism of Alexandria and other cities or communities, and established communes in the Egyptian desert valleys to be with the

Lord—and to be away from people (!)—to go be with Jesus in the desert. You may admire their writings and spirit in works such as *The Sayings of the Desert Fathers*. This movement had influence upon all Christendom to follow them in some way especially with their emphasis on solitude, rhythm of prayer, mindfulness, penance, spiritual direction.

St. Benedict (480-550), Italian founder of Western monasticism and generator of communal meditation and penance, emphasized silence, humility and especially "listening with the heart," while reading the Bible (usually the Psalms) and chanting them with devotion. He set up a system to cultivate internalization of the Word so God's word would be "living within the disciple." *Ora et labora*, prayer and work, one of the mottoes of Benedictines, stresses the rhythm of prayer and gentle pace one should live one life by, never neglecting ongoing prayer and mindfulness.

St. Augustine (354-430) is the great North African saint who searched for and stressed the experience of God (as well as orthodox theology, after experiencing literally just about everything and everyone else). He also sought the balance between the immanent and transcendent Lord—God above and within us. For St. Augustine, God as Trinity is "implanted" within each person, especially manifested within the three faculties of the memory, will, and intellect. He can be an excellent model of balance for us today as he was both active in the world (as bishop) and also as a contemplative.

Pseudo-Dionysius (Syria fourth century) is the anonymous author of influential works like *The Mystical Theology* and *The Heavenly Hierarchy*. He was perhaps a monk, who affected much of Western Christendom's spiritual legacy with the *via negativa*—a way of seeking God that states what God is not (He is not finite/not contained/not fully graspable, etc.), contrasted with the *via affirmative* (what God is, "God is Love"—Jn. 4:16). Also found in or from Pseudo-Dionysius are the classification of general stages of the spiritual life—illumination, purgation, and union—wherein the soul progresses with God and this "spiritual roadmap" affected the East and West in great ways until this day.

ST. BERNARD (1090-1153) and the Trappists, as some of his monk-followers are known, are a movement and outgrowth of late Benedictines, stressing an intimate-prayerful love relationship with God, poverty and work, levels of prayer and steps of meditation, and which blossomed forth seemingly infinite glosses of the Bible commentary.

ST. FRANCIS OF ASSISI (1182-1226) lived in Umbria, Italy, and began his own religious order of prayer and service (notice the balance) stressing God's creation through poetry and praise. He was also known for his revival of the somewhat medieval corrupt church and his contemplation of the passion of God. He received the stigmata, Christ's wounds imprinted upon his body like Christ's, which denotes interior identification with the Lord's Passion for which we should all strive.

ST. DOMINIC (1170-1221) was the Spanish founder of the Dominican order, a contemporary of St. Francis and also a mendicant (one who begs while walking and preaching). He stressed the truth of God's Word both in the Bible and Sacred Tradition (Catholic Church teachings) and its application to daily life. The handy, spiritual-pragmatic prayers of Dominicans—*contemplata aliis tradere*—means we should "give away the fruits of one's contemplation." According to holy legend and tradition, Dominic received the Rosary (as revealed from Heaven) and this changed his whole fledgling mission in France to success.

DEVOTIO MODERNA is a movement developed during the 1300s and for a hundred years after. Gerard Groote (1340-1384), a German spiritual devotee, and others formed a "pious movement" of laity and clergy alike. Stressing piety, spiritual reading, and emphasis upon the heart (versus overly intellectual analysis), the movement spawned other spiritual groups like the Beguines and Beghards that inspired laymen and women's movements to live a more serious Christian life. Thomas Kempis (1370-1471), is best known amidst this spiritual stream, and his work *The Imitation of Christ* is vastly popular and influential even today. It stresses sentiment, simplicity, conformity to the suffering Christ, humility and penance and simple way of living.

THE CLOUD OF UNKNOWING (14th century), an anonymous medieval work, probably by an English monk, is a classic, simple, and understandable book on the soul and the desire to lead an interior life, mental prayer, and simple focus upon God, with usage of a word or phrase that helps one from distractions and leads toward deepening prayer. It also counsels the abandonment of definitive notions and knowledge "about" God and, rather, surrender into the "unknown-ness" in which we may more purely perceive and receive God's true nature.

ST. IGNATIUS (1491-1556) is the founder of the Jesuits, a teaching and missionary order. They stress *contemplativus in actionis*—"contemplative in action." A life of discipleship is first to be prayerful, contemplative, centered in God, and then active. Another Jesuit motto is "finding God in all things" which links our inner essence of prayer to an outer, active life.

ST. TERESA OF AVILA (1515-1582), the "mystic wonder woman," opened more than 70 monasteries across Spain, revived a moribund Carmelite contemplative order, and wrote tons of works on the spiritual life, most famously, *The Interior Castle*, intimating that she joined to, and loved Christ, who is at the center of our interior lives, waiting within amidst all disturbances and attachments. She blazed a new contemplative path and inspired the old one of mental prayer and meditation; codified many terms of interior life (recollection, prayer of quiet, etc.) She offers us great themes and practices as the journey within, offering the option between dilly-dallying versus real interior prayer, detachment and personal relationship with Christ the Lord.

St. John of the Cross (1542-1591), a friend of St. Teresa of Avila after she pegged him as a "co-reformer" for the Carmelite order, is known as "Mystic Doctor." Why? Because he systematically and supernaturally plumbed the depths of the soul through his writings and prescriptions, what ails us all—attachments that lead to necessary purgations of "dark nights" as well as how to heal through one's own active efforts, and God's passive purgations, through a cleansing wherein we can come more freely to God. In essence, if God is All, then all (gods) must be swept from the soul's entanglements in the path to union. Although known for his meekness, he was imprisoned for his faith and in that very midst formed *The Spiritual Canticle*—showing us that out of evil comes great good. These are all lessons for us today!

The French school of spirituality, inspired by Jean-Jacques Olier (1608-1657), emphasizes personal closeness to Jesus Christ, mental prayer with emphasis upon the role of the heart in meditation, the importance of feeling and emotion. In contrast, the Jesuit school promotes the intellect and thinking in meditation. As meditators we need both affective and intellective ingredients to cultivate in our deeper prayer.

MODERN CONTEMPLATIVE DIMENSIONS

St. Thérèse of Lisieux (1873-1897) and her classic work, *The Story of a Soul*, exemplify the universal desire for holiness as well as the practice of spiritual simplicity, meditation, and abandonment to God in ordinary, daily things, and also interior recollection.

THE SOUL OF THE APOSTOLATE by the Benedictine Dom Chautard is a hugely influential book that was published as a reminder to "worker (activist) priests" and any busied Christians whose active works (whether in the parish, at home, or in the world) must always be based in a meditative spiritual life. Ultimately, we "activists" will burn out or break down if we do not base our lives first in prayer and interior life. He wrote, "We must never leave the God of works for the works of God," and quoted our Lord's saying: "What does it profit a man, if he gain the whole world and suffer the loss of his own soul?" (Mk. 8:36).

VATICAN COUNCIL II (1962-1965), convoked by Pope St. John XXIII to stimulate and update the Catholic Church in the modern world, called for Catholics to deeper prayer and, to the surprise of some, mentions "contemplation" in its various document many times, thus emphasizing the interior life is at the heart of being a Christian.

THOMAS MERTON (1915-1968) was a fabled Trappist monk who was initially very secular. After his conversion to Catholicism, he eventually grew into to monasticism, scribed many writings of meditation, contemplation, and spirituality and was a popularizer of the interior life. While known for his social commentary and peace efforts, he nonetheless emphasized the spiritual life as a basis for activism and re-connecting with God.

THE 1960S brought a lot of spiritually questionable (read: relativistic) stuff to the faith but also stimulated a lot of interior movements—and also the conversation of East and West, between Buddhism, Hinduism, and Christianity, which now affects interreligious dialogue—and by which many have become syncretized (inappropriately integrating foreign elements to Christina faith).

EAST MEETS WEST—SYNCRETISM

Here are some influences and factors of which you can be aware:

HINDUISM developed more than 1,000 years before Christ. This vast religious system originated in northern India through the Aryan peoples and manifested in various spiritual philosophies and practices, eventually consolidating into the loosely related system of polytheism called Hinduism (which includes yoga and its many schools). Like Catholicism, Hinduism is a spiritual and folkway culture and has proved miraculously adept at adapting to various other societies and cultures, as well as integrating itself within other diverse spiritual and philosophical beliefs.

BUDDHISM developed from Hinduism and, like Christianity, became a critique of "the old school" of Hinduism, by Siddhartha Gautama, the Buddha. It emphasizes in this case life as suffering because of desires, and liberation from this by meditation, enlightenment-nirvana, and selflessness.

TAOISM, the philosophy of the classic spiritual, *Tao Te Ching*, (translated variously as "*The Way and Virtue*"), is usually attributed to the sage Lao Tzu (605-531 BC). It stresses passivity and non-egoic-doing while learning about the subtle ways of the Tao (spiritual force-energy in the world) and not impressing ego upon the world or others against "naturalist ways."

NEW AGE refers to the nebulous combining of Eastern spiritual elements with Western philosophy, psychology, and self-help into a loose system, which adherents and teachers choose and practice at will. It is basically monistic (there is one being of all reality, usually emphasizing Spirit as non-personal). It sometimes de-emphasizes morality and is sometimes non-religious, favoring a "spiritual, but not religious" approach.

continue page 16 »

MINDFULNESS refers to a burgeoning and somewhat nebulous secular spirituality of being present at each moment or in the current action or to oneself in meditation and is usually based on Eastern meditation techniques, but can also be used by Catholics in various ways.

There are many other spiritualities (Kabbala, Native American, "environmentalism," etc.) that we cannot cover here. Suffice to say, many "spiritualists" today syncretistically link these various influences into their particular brand of meditation or spirituality and influence others, including Catholicism and Christianity. Others, meanwhile, reject out-of-hand any intercourse with anything foreign to traditional Christianity, especially denying this as "spiritual dabbling" and new ageism. It seems there are a lot of extremes!

While there are seeds of truth in various religions in the world, as Vatican II suggests, we must also, as the Council further asserts, be aware of dangers and errors in other philosophies alien to us. Let's take the middle position of moderation in things Eastern, between the extremes of total rejection and naïve acceptance. We can learn a lot from others when it is proper, appropriate and when we are sure in our own faith. We can avoid syncretism—combining, blithely, elements of the world that shouldn't be blended into Christian faith or practice, while also avoiding fundamentalism—the idea that all cultures and/ or secular elements are our automatic "enemy" to Western, biblical Christianity. Catholicism is balanced between these extremes and is thus incarnational basing itself in reality and natural law truths.

CENTERING PRAYER

Centering Prayer is a recent spiritual movement that is basically a combination of *lectio divina* or sacred reading and meditation. In this movement the soul focuses on a word, repeating it as an aspiration or mantra, and this perhaps leading to deeper forms of prayer-contemplation. While it is a nascent movement like all things modern and trending, one must discern the adherents as well as teachers of it closely.

YOUR STATE IN LIFE

So, after this brief history of the meditative life, you may see there is enough spiritual "grist for the mill" for your soul to feed upon! Okay, I know—you're not a monk or nun, and you can't always go to a church or flee to a cloister, especially with kids nipping at you or work calling you—but you are called to an interior life—of prayer and spiritual conversation with God no matter who or what you are.

There is, obviously, a deep and rich source for practical disciplines like silence, stillness, inner reflection and composure, witnessed and penned by both clerical and lay writers that you, now, are called to that same interior life in whatever way you can. Christians through the centuries have forged a path of meditation and God calls everyone to a more internal and deep way of living.

So, on the one hand, you must seek this in your life or you'll never get it—no one will give it to you, and, as a matter of fact, more will try to take it away from you! On the other hand, you need to realize that while having this spiritual zeal, you have other duties to fulfill that form the main part of your "state in life"—whether as a married or single person or like me, clergy member.

This is a delicate and daily balance—between striving for prayer time and fulfilling your duties. You have obligations the monk does not and so must live out your own lay responsibilities while also (and here's that balance-thing again) never neglecting your own prayer life. But, a caveat: some lay persons obviously take themselves off the hook, precisely because they are laypersons, not monks or nuns and so become what we could call "spiritual slackers."

Remember, especially these days as described above, all the business people and corporations that are teaching mindfulness; all the lay persons now enacting *lectio divina*; all the devout souls joining third order lay movements to partake of what clergy and nuns are doing in their callings.

So, find that sacred place and time, daily, especially within yourself wherever you are, to meet and converse with God. Remember the basics of meditation/*lectio* are:

- *Read* (Observe)
- *Reflect* (Think)
- *Respond* (Converse with God)

And:

- *Picture within* a meditation subject or scene
- *Think about* it by using your brain
- *Thank him* by using your heart

Hear Our Lord calling you: "Come away by yourselves, to a deserted place, and rest awhile" (Mk. 6:31) Do you hear the call? Are you going to him in meditation? Are you making a sincere response with your life?

SOME PRELIMINARY SUGGESTIONS

In this art and discipline of meditation here are some suggestions:

- Don't get hung up on words or descriptions I give about meditation. The mind will follow what the heart does naturally.

- The more important thing is to pray, meditate, practically, heart-fully.

- Pray and meditate every day for ten minutes or more.

- Cultivate this discipline for at least one month and then expand it into more time devoted to meditation.

- Meditation means a faith-focus, inward loving concentration and cultivation and a regular practice of this over time. In other words, you are developing a love relationship with God.

- Meditation is not an end in itself but a loving discipline leading you to a deeper relationship with God the Trinity, especially by way of internal practice.

You will encounter the phrase "interior life" often in this book, and it basically means both the discipline of meditation, the practice of stillness and silence, the heart and head centered on God and his ways as well as a preservation of such from excessive internal and external stimuli.

Thus, an interior life involves, positively, practicing concentration and love within and, "negatively," guarding your soul from excessive, internal (self) and external stimuli which drain and addict you, thus compromising the inner, delicate life God has for you. There is a lot of detail here, so read slowly, ponder the various words and meanings, as they will indicate our way forward in this book and address the fact so many today are attached or addicted to so many things in life they are seldom still or silent. Unfortunately, this includes many Christians!

CHAPTER TWO

WHAT IS MEDITATION?

"...AFTER THE FIRE, A LIGHT SILENT SOUND..."
– 1 KG. 19:12

The main premise of this book is we all need more prayer and meditation in our lives. *More God*—if you will—realized through inward prayer and a consistent interior life. We also need pragmatic prayer—concretely connecting with God instead of just thinking about him, or reading prayers, or consuming theology books on mysticism (like I used to do). In other words, we need an *I-want-the-meal- not-just-the-menu* approach to spirituality.

This *Little Book on Meditation* is intended to help guide you in the actual practice of meditation—God-centered prayer. We all need help in the art of praying itself, encountering God and, in particular, through stillness and silence in his presence. This seems to be lost in our Western Christian world. Perhaps this is why some folks (including myself in past times) flee to the East—New Age, Buddhism, etc.—to get to *praxis*, the actual practice of prayer.

Yet, as implied previously, so many today want spirituality without (Western) religion because, allegedly, it hasn't delivered practical help or meditative disciplines—at least that's the perception. Or Christianity is perceived as "overburdened" with too much morality or dry-as-dust dogma. This mindset sees religion as stale and without "sweet God-experiences." All commandments and no creativity: How boring!

IN SEARCH OF AN "EXPERIENTIAL SPIRITUALITY."

Rightly or wrongly, haven't we Catholics and non-Catholic Christians been too much about business, buildings, and bake sales, and too little about religious practice, prayer, and spirituality? However, when you think about it or dig into the history of our faith, we do have jewels of famous works such as *The Sayings of the Desert Fathers* from ancient Egypt; *The Mind's Ascent to God* by St. Bonaventura; *Introduction to the Devout Life* by St. Francis de Sales, with its emphasis on aesthetic training in basic spirituality; and *The Graces of the Interior Life* by Augustine Poulin which, with delineations on the stages of prayer and obstacles and graces therein, is a modern classic, a compilation of mysticism. These works are direct helps to a practical prayer life and illustrate the beauty of Western Christianity and the invitation to a deeper union with God.

Often, in my search for meditation, I've been confounded by a lack of instruction. However, upon closer observation, you might notice that Jesus along with the Holy Spirit gives instruction, saying, "When you pray, go into your inner room, close the door, and pray to your Father in secret" (Mt. 6:6). The Lord is fostering an interior life. Are you following? Let us do that now by the practical prayer and scriptural prescription: "Be still and know I am God" (Ps. 46: 11). In other words, be still anytime and anywhere and sense God's presence.

A DEEP BIBLICAL LESSON

Before we get into the "meat" of meditation-matter, I'd like to reflect for a moment on the seminal lesson of Elijah, the Old Testament prophet who is searching for God—just like us—amidst all the "fireworks" of life:

> *He got up, ate, and drank; then strengthened by that food, he walked forty days and forty nights to the mountain of God, Horeb. There he came to a cave, where he took shelter. But the word of the Lord came to him: "Why are you here, Elijah?" He answered: "I have been most zealous for the Lord, the God of hosts, but the Israelites have forsaken your covenant. They have destroyed your altars and murdered your prophets by the sword. I alone remain, and they seek to take my life." Then the Lord said: "Go out and stand on the mountain before the Lord; the Lord will pass by." There was a strong and violent wind rending the mountains and crushing rocks before the Lord—but the Lord was not in the wind; after the wind, an earthquake—but the Lord was not in the earthquake; after the earthquake, fire—but the Lord was not in the fire; after the fire, a light silent sound. When he heard this, Elijah hid his face in his cloak and went out and stood at the entrance of the cave. A voice said to him, "Why are you here, Elijah?" (1 Kg. 19: 8-12)*

Another translation says that he "sojourned" for forty nights. Sojourned means to make a journey. Life is a journey and so is prayer.

Through prayer and meditation, we become purified and more able to love and know God, but it takes time and patience. The previous reference to "nights" indicates a deep, purified, elevated, and difficult journey into God (in other words, it is never simple or automatic).

We may also infer from the text that we humans naturally seek God in explicit, loud, overt, and sensual ways as Elijah sought him, through "earthquakes" and "fires." This is natural. Meditation, however, teaches us to wait on the Lord, to go through and beyond these external, sometimes distracting attractions, and find God within, in the subtle, gentle breezes. We may summarize this helpful text as an illustration of impulsiveness versus internalization. Are you going to "get" God through the sensual, instant fires and earthquakes of life (impulses), or through disciplined prayer and meditation (interiorization)?

"SPIRITUAL AND THE SPIRIT"

Here are the extremes in meditation to avoid: pacifism, where we just sit back and God does all the work, and Pelagianism, where we're doing all the work. Pelagianism is named after Pelagius, an early, errant bishop who opposed the Church and basic Christian teachings and believed that personal effort alone saves and enlightens us. The Church condemned this idea, stressing that all Christians believe in the Holy Spirit as a divine person of the Trinity, the "Sanctifier," the One who makes us holy. God makes us holy; we can't do it by ourselves. In other words, we need God to make us godly, to make us holy. We need to pray to the Holy Spirit to help us, sanctify us, to help us be still, focused, inwardly disciplined in our prayer and meditation and active lives. While we all need the virtues of effort and zeal, we need rely more primarily on God's grace. Holiness and following God and meditation are a combination both of our acting-striving and cooperation with God's grace.

Jesus Christ himself, in his constitution, shows us that he is two natures: true God and true man. Likewise, we need two elements, nature and grace, human zeal and divine assistance, in holiness. We must ask the Holy Spirit to help us become holy, assist our efforts, and complement our spiritual striving—in essence, to help us "spiritualize" our lowly selves.

IN A NUTSHELL

Basically, this *Little Book* will help you in the methods of meditation by way of "Three I's": Instruction, Imagination, Interiorization. We will thus cover Instruction on stillness and silence, Imagination to "picture within" images of religious devotion, and Interiorization, internalizing all the lessons learned.

Everyone has the capacity for prayer and perhaps even for meditation, but does everyone try to *realize* this capability and calling? Of course not. We're sometimes more obsessed with sports, possessions, work, multitasking, and getting ahead in life. Therefore, in the first chapter of this book, we discussed some of the essentials of meditation: stillness, silence, grace and focus, and how these can offset the humdrum of an overly busy lifestyle. We will now acquaint you with meditation itself as understood by Western Christianity and, in particular, Roman Catholicism (our focus will be narrow as there are many varieties of meditation). You don't have to be Catholic (or a Christian, for that matter) to understand meditation or begin practicing what I am encouraging—just be open to joining in on the spiritual path!

THE LESSON OF ST. PAUL

Okay, since we got that simple-yet-complicated theology history and lesson down, let us return once more to St. Paul, who gives us this observation-admonition in a famous "mystical passage": "All of us, gazing with unveiled face on the glory of the Lord, are being transformed into the same image, from glory to glory, as from the Lord, who is the Spirit" (2 Cor. 3:18). This is a classic text of mystical literature, from St. Paul himself. It illustrates many important mystical-meditational points:

1. We need, in meditation, to strip ourselves from excessive, often external, extras that burden and weigh upon us and our spiritual pursuit.

2. We must focus on the glory of the Lord—not ourselves, even our own sins and "stripping process" but, rather, on the glory of God!

3. The spiritual life is a transformational process, with God as the main "actor" and transformer.

4. This process is thus "from glory to glory," which equates to stages and years of perseverance going ever more upward and deeper and higher God-likeness.

5. This is because this transformational process is from God who is pure Spirit and we are dust and earthy—so far lower than He is!

In essence, this biblical passage demonstrates the classic threefold way of spiritual life: illumination, purification, and union.

Let's break that down that Pauline saying and simplify it into distinct-but-related parts:

> *"All of us, gazing with unveiled faces*
> *On the glory of the Lord,*
> *Are being transformed into the same image,*
> *From glory to glory,*
> *As from the Lord, who is the Spirit."*

This is the purpose of Catholic-Christian meditation and this *Little Book*—transformation by, and into God, especially through prayerful meditation as both a desire and discipline of our lives.

Enough of the talk, let's "walk the walk," as we move on to the basics of meditation.

GOING DEEPER

"Forgetfulness of creation,
Remembrance of the Creator,
Attention to what is within,
Loving the Beloved."
—St. John of the Cross.

Christians are different from those in the world or, at least, should be—if they practice what they preach and preach what they actually practice. It's what Jesus did—demonstrate continual Presence of God: "The Kingdom of God is among you" (Lk. 17:21). Not only did he go to the temple as a good Jew, but he went away to the lake, mountain, and desert. He did this, not only to "get away from it all," but also to be an example for us of what we should do—to get away *to the All*. If Jesus had to get away from us humans (!) and human activity, then what about us humans and our needs?

I was recently visiting with my home pastor, Fr. Paul. He was radiant at age 82, after 37 years as pastor at my home parish in Maryland, and some 50 years of priesthood. We discussed his upcoming retirement, and he said so keenly, "Jack, I'm ready for *being* after so many years of *doing*."

That's what meditation is about—being vs. doing. Or better yet, proper be-ing which leads to rhythmic doing; in the right order, they're complimentary. The emphasis in meditation is on surrender to God—be-ing—so we may be balanced in our activities. Priests, parish priests especially, are so used to doing, fixing, adapting, pragmatically solving so many different things, it's difficult to stop, to be still and actually focus and meditate. And yet, that's our job—or, at least it's in our job description, to pray more deeply. But my pastor, this wise priest, was practicing just that and showing me exactly what to do in my own life, too! Remember, it's not just for priests—proper being leads to proper doing for everyone.

When you get down to it, prayer or meditation is simply sitting and focusing and disciplining oneself to become aware of God's life within. We Christians can talk a good talk, but don't always walk the walk of spirituality and meditation. We sometimes have this "inner avoidance syndrome"—a sometimes vague denial of the need to deepen our spirituality within. Therefore, we may (choose one): rationalize, stall, stay in control, take the easy way out, trivialize God, boil Christianity down to a slacker version, or just give up. Thus, we need an antidote for all this in the cultivation of an interior life. We've got it all in Catholicism and Christianity: spiritual treasures of theory and practice in Christianity and the West to help slow down and prayerfully reflect.

LEARNING FROM PROS

One time, after a long wedding service (I know I shouldn't describe a Catholic service as "long," but…), I whisked out of the church after the nice ceremony. I had one thing on my mind: to watch the World Cup soccer finals being played the very afternoon that the bride and groom had the gall to schedule their wedding at the same time—Ugggh!

I raced down the street and stopped into several stores looking for a TV. I'm sure it must have looked interesting: priest carrying flowing robes, running, plunging his head from store to store, manically asking for "The Soccer Game." (P.S.: I also had to go to the bathroom after that long service: now I know how my parishioners feel!) Finally, after four failed attempts of finding "The Game," I entered the next store and looked around. No one was nearby, but, wait, there was someone there, or was there? Was it a body, a person? Whatever "it" was, it was in the back of an aisle, motionless. So I spoke, "Hello!" No answer. Then I tried, "Excuse me. …" Still no answer. Okay, now "Operation Desperation." I tried again to see if it was actually a person back there, blurting out: "Can I watch on this computer—a soccer game?" Then it seemed to me that the object I saw was a real person who was seemingly bowing and then lying on the floor. Strange. What was going on?

It soon became apparent: I saw the rug on the floor and noticed the Middle-Eastern features of the man. I got it. He was Muslim and was praying his mandatory prayers. He was transfixed in his meditation. When he was finished praying, he got up, rolled his rug methodically, and came over and welcomed me.

Wow! I totally forgot about the soccer game at this point—and became embarrassed, and then thought: *Dedication!* I wondered if I could get that focus, that spiritual attunement in my spiritual life. This was a lesson to me, one who preaches a lot about "public faith" and practicing your religion in the marketplace without being embarrassed—this was essential news that I need to actually be as deep, concentrated and spiritually disciplined as the man I met that day. I know I can meditate; yet, especially lately, I get so easily distracted. I used to be more inclined into deeper meditation and concentration but had slacked off in the last year. That man's example inspired me to return to a deeper form of prayer.

I saw an aspect of meditation in that man's prayerful actions—stillness, an element as we stated in the Introduction as one of the many necessary ingredients of meditation. Meditation is basically loving God—and being loved by him—in stillness, silence, and through an interior life we all need to develop. Read that last sentence again. "Interior life"—a classical Christian phrase of yesteryear, is something that is both seemingly alien to modern life (with all our communication, busyness and activities) but also freeing it (in other words, we're no longer addicted to outward, external things or activities). Simply put, meditation can be described with these three phases:

- Picture within
- Think about
- Thank him

TYPES OF MEDITATION

How do we acquire an interior life? Broadly speaking there are three ways of meditating that will help us and, to simplify things, we may call these *text, image,* and *word,* or respectively, reading, picturing, and aspiration.

The first kind of meditation begins in words—we meditate upon words of actual writing. And so to begin this way of meditation (called *lectio,* meaning writing), we might read a Bible verse or brief spiritual passage and use that for the basis of meditation. The second kind of meditation can be called "image" or "visual way," which begins either outside yourself—looking at a picture or an icon, or by visualizing within yourself an image or event.

The last form of meditation is a memorized word or phrase, mantra, or aspiration that we reverently repeat or say within.

These three forms include all the major ways of meditating and have an "object" (or content to think about) as their center. To further delineate, these forms of meditation either begin externally—outside the meditator and then become internalized (thinking within), or the meditation begins within and becomes even deeper from that starting point.

Thus, regarding the three modes of meditation, we can sum it up in these steps:
  • Imagining
  • Thinking
  • Thanking

FIRST STEP: The faculty or power of imagination, or phantasy, from ancient roots in the Latin and Greek, means "to make visible," and this is one of the most important steps of meditation. This power of the soul composes a scene within "the mind's eye" (to "picture within"), either from a selected text, word, or image, and this becomes the "primary content" of the meditation, called the "object," whether involving Jesus, the Virgin Mary, or just about any religious image or, alternatively, another image such as a creation scene of the world that we use for spiritual purposes. (As we shall see and explain later, just about any image is fodder for meditation.) The more concrete, real, sensual, and colorful this object, the better as these are enticements and tangible attachments for the intellect that allow our fleeting minds to fix on and think about. St. Ignatius counseled his Jesuits to enter into scenes in meditation and use all the senses in developing the "internal picture" with imagination. For instance, while meditating on the Lord Jesus' birthday at Christmas, we may enter the stable itself. Smell the donkeys and hay nearby. See the mist of the breathing animals and humans in the coolness of the night. Be there in the scene. Appreciate the Virgin's adoration of the Lord with your heart and eyes. Look at St. Joseph's fatherly care. Hear the animals moving. Touch the divine baby's soft skin. In other words, get into it!

SECOND STEP: The intellect should *extract* from the scene or object some content, or major themes to think about. This stage of meditation primarily uses the head, the thinker. While we think and use the intellect in this step, we should not overly intellectualize. Meditation is not only a "head game" or "Einsteinian" trip of who can think the fastest or highest or most ethereally. No, meditation is simply basic thinking about the spiritual subject matter within, and then…

THE THIRD STEP: You now *respond* to the fruits gained from intellectual thinking by giving thanks. This stage employs the heart and involves emotions, getting engaged in the subject movingly instead of just intellectualizing and creating flighty ideas. Perhaps we could call it "emotionalizing the intellect" or "feeling the thoughts."

In short-form, this is what we mean:
Picture within means formulate an internal image of your content of

meditation. Be "fleshy" and real and visceral as your mind-intellect will better be able to feed upon this, which is especially needed in the early stages of a meditator's life.

Think about means use your head and wits and mind to conjure up any thoughts and ideas about the picture within, the content of meditation.

Thank him means use your heart, sentiments, and feelings to respond to whatever you thought or internally "saw" in the meditation.

This three-stage approach, which is millennia old, lasts and passes on for many reasons—and you are called to discipline yourself in this classic school of spirituality

We will further delineate these aspects of meditation more deeply as we continue.

PRAYER AND MEDITATION

The Catechism of the Catholic Church gives the classic definition of prayer: "the lifting of the mind and heart to God" (CCC 2558, quoting St. John Damascene). That, too, is a definition of meditation—a relationship involving both mind and heart given to God in stillness and silence. We should not lose this most delicate balance in our spiritual lives and the modern world. We need the balance between thinking and feeling, and we need to explore both of these in our pursuit of holiness. This is what leads to holiness! This is what it means to be Christian and a spiritual soul.

We read, further, in the Catechism:

> *Meditation is, above all, a quest. The mind seeks to understand the why and how of the Christian life in order to adhere and respond to what the Lord is asking (CCC 2705).*

> *Meditation engages thought, imagination, emotion, and desire. This mobilization of faculties is necessary to deepen our*

convictions of faith, prompt the conversion of our heart, and strengthen our will to follow Christ. Christian prayer tries above all to meditate on the mysteries of Christ, as in Lectio Divina or the rosary. This form of prayerful reflection is of great value, but Christian prayer should go further: to the knowledge of the love of the Lord Jesus, to union with him (CCC 2708).

Meditation is, then, the very worship of God. This might seem self-evident (or, might not to some), but we must note that with the many forms of meditation these days, the First Commandment should always be first: "Thou shalt have no other gods before me" (Ex. 20:3-5)—and this means worship of God. That includes and guards against making the self a god, too, which some fashionable spiritualities and meditation systems promote. In America, especially, we need to be aware of this with all the self-help and abundant life ministries promoting and maximizing self-messages to worship God , whether implicitly or explicitly.

I once heard a priest speaking to a clergy group and he stressed the importance of self by seeking inner peace, calm, the ability of the self to be in the present moment, and the au courant phraseology, "the ability to be loved by God." Now, if these "selfisms" are not kept subservient to the all-important command to worship God, then we will get lost in endless self-searching and fulfillment, and spiritual navel-gazing. If God is not first and foremost as worthy of adoration and honor, and is the reason we meditate, we will inevitably go off course.

The main goal of prayer is to raise the mind and heart *to God*. When we honor him first, then the fruits of prayer—self-discovery and so forth—will be logical outcomes, not first principles or preoccupations. We shouldn't become neo-Pelagians—where prayer and spirituality are all about *our* works and *our* efforts, with an excessive focus on self-healing and self-centered egoism.

Another helpful example of God-centered focus comes from St. John of the Cross. Through his deep and continual searching into the self before God, he showed us the need for purification—giving us an invaluable "religious map" of our interior lives but also illustrating that this self-discovery process should be done for God's glory and not selfishness. In essence, "first things" (worshiping God) leads to "secondary things" (fulfilling self).

In *The Interior Castle*, St. Teresa of Avila defined Christian meditation as follows: "By meditation I mean prolonged reasoning with the understanding, *in this way*. We begin by thinking of the favor which God bestowed upon us by giving us his only Son, and we do not stop there, but proceed to consider the mysteries of his whole glorious life." (Sixth Mansion, Chapter 7, 1)

Notice, meditation is more about God and his favors to us who humbles himself to descend to us. Secondarily, it is also about our union with him.

While in college in the early 1980s, I took a course in meditation. It was a life-changer. One of my teachers, Professor Hill, a.k.a. "Zen Santa Claus" as he looked like both a Zen master and Santa Claus (with his long white beard and affability), introduced our class and me to the treasures of the East and the West's mysticism and philosophy—along with intentional spiritual practice, journaling, and of course our subject du jour, meditation.

We studied classics such as those of St. John of the Cross, St. Teresa of Avila, and St. Thérèse of Lisieux. Then, we forayed into *Three Pillars of Zen* by Phillip Kapleau, Hindu poetry and a whole variety of Eastern-mystical texts. I really got into the subjects from the get-go. We did research, papers, and, of course, actual "practice." Practice, meaning meditation, was very challenging. We were required to do ten minutes a day, which doesn't seem like much until you actually try it and commit to doing it for three months. It was difficult at first, but I did it or, eventually, was able to do it and, just as important, still do it. That little ten minutes back then grew into the current prayer routine of two hours that I practice daily.

Always remember—small spiritual baby steps lead toward tall, big steps, just like everything else in life.

Back then, I was very drawn to the new things I was learning about meditation and spiritual seeking and journaling. It all helped me into a beautiful new world and, just as significantly, out of a dark one of drugs and depression into which I had slipped. Meditation affected the arc of my entire life—maybe one of the reasons why I'm now a priest. Notice this didn't occur in the church or monastery or Christian workshop but within a state-run university! Yes, your tax dollars helped me become a priest—a good example of church-state cooperation and, along with the philosophy professor, all these fostered my spiritual love for interior recollection.

Now, let us get back to the "word picture" aspect of meditation. Imagine of one of those snow globes you see on someone's fireplace mantle. When you shake up the glass container, it looks furiously hectic and enervated within. There's a lot of snow spewing about because of the shaking action. However, when you set the snow globe down, all the snow-stress becomes settled and you can see the pretty little town or gingerbread house, calm and welcoming. Our minds and bodies are like this and so are our lives. We need to physically stop, to still that which overly affects our minds and still our souls so that a transparency, a clearness comes—and so God may more easily grace our inner being.

Following along with this illustration, I recall meeting a priest one time—a saint, according to some, and, after talking about various life-issues, interests, and activities, he said, "No, you don't have to do anything for your priestly identity. You only have *to be*. There's so much stress today in doing in our ministries, accomplishing, producing. But we priests especially have to remember that in our being, the Father's image and Jesus is impressed within us."

"URGE TO MERGE"

People do it all the time—follow the "urge to merge." It's a desire and a push to become one with someone or something, in a physical or mental union. This urge is stimulated within ourselves through relationships, food obsessions, or sexual lusts or it is fed by external, societal tendencies, such as endlessly entrancing TVs, or promotion of materialism, or the plain old feeling of "we all want to be part of something bigger." We're all made for togetherness and oneness and until we find that, we will always be searching for it and experimenting in one way or another for it.

Think of the "urge to merge" and the good vibes you get from this, and so let's explore more deeply how this phenomenon is innate and how it affects meditation. Here are some examples:

Relationships: you see someone, you are attracted, you follow that desire and eventually you "merge with them." How many rock 'n' roll anthems, country love songs, cheesy poems and mystical ballads do you need to hear and read, to illustrate this—the desire for relationship-merger-bliss?! Once again, the elements are common and universal-desire, seeking-pursuit, finding-merger.

Drugs: whether illegal or prescription drugs, or alcohol, the incredible drug abuse phenomenon in our country nowadays testifies to how our society is obviously and obtusely manifesting the perennial urge to merge and seek pleasure.

TV: the American entertainment and film industry (and Bollywood in India) foist and foment narratives of merging through a (choose one or more): a romantic / dramatic / adventurous / time-machine-transporting storyline; and, usually, they perpetuate escaping from everyday life.

Well, amidst all these, meditation is about a merger also—a divine union. Simply remember to practice through meditation to become one with the Son. Jesus calls us: "Behold, I stand at the door and knock. If anyone hears my voice and opens the door, [then] I will enter his house

36

and dine with him, and he with me" (Rev. 3:20). Meditation is opening the door to this divine merger, oneness with Jesus Christ.

Here is a "spiritual equation" to illustrate the "urge-merge process": Desire + Searching + Finding = Merger

Briefly, let's look at those elements and apply them to meditation.

The *desire* in all human beings is for oneness.

The desire may be an individual's subtle or explicit prowling for objects, possessions, and people in the world around him/her.

Finding is his/her individual "answer" of what is a fulfilling union— and there may be many "findings."

Merger can either be authentic or superficial union and hopefully it is with God.

So, in meditation, we seek and find the heart's desire for the merger— "mystical union." Catholicism and Christianity have always taught this but today we need to re-emphasize it and, perhaps, "re-market the brand," as they say. The ultimate purpose of "The Brand"—Christianity— is that everything is meant to be or can be a way to union with God. This is called the "path of sanctification"—being in the world of everyday life and a way of union with God through relationship whether in meditation or through active life. Meditation is the ongoing and foreshadowing merger with God and soul in oneness. We should practice it daily now and look forward to it more fully, finally in Heaven. We shall enter this union *if* we choose to enter into a merger with God and the interior life of the soul now.

We all have an urge to merge and Christians find this merger and union through faith and meditation. Here are some who have "answered" the urge to merge through prayer and meditation:

- St. Augustine famously prayed in his autobiographical book, "The Confessions": "You (God) were within me, but I was outside." He led a life of meditation—and led others to it.

- Ancients and medievalists have described within us a union point with God as the "spark of the soul," the *scintilla animae*, "divine spark," and also as "temple of the soul." We all have these and should uncover them as they are the most real part of ourselves.

- St. Catherine of Siena discovered this urging and finding as the internal cloister. Because she had 22 brothers and sisters with whom to compete, she famously pled to God and struggled to find peace and quiet somewhere in her life and surroundings. But God told her there was an "inner chapel" within her soul to go to and find peace. This was the beginning of her mystical merger and spiritual ascent and deeper life.

Warning: All of these sensual "sparks" and messages just described don't occur all the time, within ourselves, when we meditate. We're likely going to have a lot of boredom and trials along the way. However, through perseverance and discipline, our souls are designed to create a kind of "inner Imax theater" of sight and sound-sensuality to stimulate the soul to develop our relationship with God and meditation. We experience some of these sensual experiences in the daily world, externally, and they may be faint or faithful hints of The Real Encounter and Union with God! We need to follow then the "merger process" from external to internal, lower to higher, perseveringly. We need to "ignite the spark" daily, in our own meditation and make this Godly merger real, sensual and ongoing.

REALISM

Okay, for another dose of realism: You're not always going to feel good prayer vibes or experience a "utopian feeling" of the universe within, or hear God directly speaking to you. Shocked? Meditation, deeper praying, doesn't automatically make you "mystical" or cause God to "appear."

Translation: You will most likely have to choose, tomorrow or in a year—to pray, making a conscious, actual choice to meditate, which contrasts with an idealistic feeling exhilarated to pray in veritable ease. So, just because you read in a book somewhere or heard how happy folks are in their meditating lives, or even hear the latest poll that shows spirituality makes people happier, remember that, like many other things in life, there's a lot of hype about spiritual things. You, instead will need to persevere, continue focusing even when it seems impossible and take the long-haul approach versus spiritual sprinting or false hopes of "everything's coming up roses." Upshot: Don't magically think meditation will always be easy. *Persevere.*

Dryness, aridity and desert experiences will likely come—and not infrequently—to all of us. After all, St. Teresa of Avila and St. Teresa of Kolkata both experienced decades of darkness and absence of consolations; however, they kept on—persevered in their spiritual and interior lives. If these great saints had troubles, don't you think you will?

So, before getting into more theory, let's simply practice a meditation now, to help us practically. *Visualize* Jesus as in that famous pious painting where he is standing outside a door of a home with a glowing lantern. Picture him knocking on *your* door. Next, *Think about* what is he doing there, now, in me, within? What does he want? Last, *Thank him.* Be grateful for him, God, coming into you in the first place, and arriving to assuage your problems and bring you salvation-healing.

Simply put, the process is to visualize, think, and give thanks. Take some time with this spiritual process in a gentle way to deepen your love of the Lord.

CHAPTER THREE

MEDITATION
AND PRAYER

"COME TO ME, ALL YOU WHO LABOR AND ARE
BURDENED, AND I WILL GIVE YOU REST"
(MT. 11:28)

Who doesn't find life wearying, at least sometimes? The more we sit in silence and stillness, in meditation with Jesus, the more we will be refreshed. It's that simple. The opposite is true, too; the more you stay on the treadmill, the more famished you will become. The choice is yours. Meditation is the option for imagination and peace, through stillness and silence.

Now let's look at three forms of prayer that will help complement our interior lives: oration, meditation, and contemplation.

If oration can be described as praying and thinking about many things (say a series of biblical scenes or mysteries of Jesus' life), or, praying out loud or with others, then meditation is inner-directed, focusing on one image or thing. The highest form of prayer, contemplation, is total rest, stillness of all mental faculties, inner and outer silence; God gracing us to rest in him alone.

Unfortunately, most people never "graduate" or mature from oration to meditation because, while meditation is difficult, Christians of all stripes either never learn meditation or do not discipline themselves to focus and be still because of our instant gratification or multi-tasking culture affecting us so contantly, as well as the "inner treadmill" that so many today seem to be on.

Basically, as maturing Christians, we are to progress in our prayer, from oration to meditation and, God willing, to contemplation—from some objects of focus and consideration to one object alone, gradually to none, receiving God himself, hopefully in contemplation.

A very simple way to meditate is what I like to refer to as "The Three R's." This is very similar to, and based upon, *lectio divina*, "divine reading" —which is usually meditation on the Word of God, usually the Bible. With the happy advent and proliferation of spiritual booklets on prayer, Mass readings, meditation, and saints lives, *lectio divina* has progressed popularly as prayerful reading of sacred texts, usually the Bible, in slow consideration, as so many now have access to the readings of the Mass and Gospels.

The Three R's are *Read, Reflect,* and *Respond*:

- Read (or, Review) the object of meditation: familiarize yourself with the text, topic or, if an image, review-visualize within the picture or icon or object. This step simply emphasizes encountering the "object"——the "what" of meditation.

- Reflect: go deeper with and within the object; think about the object within, cogitate, use your intellect, stimulate curiosity, and think about it.

- Respond: to God about the lessons or inspirations you have thought about previously—now using your heart and feelings.

That's it, in essence, the basic "spiritual skeleton" of meditation and what you minimally need to get started: Read, Reflect, and Respond.

Take ten minutes each day for a week, then go up to fifteen minutes for the second week you meditate and eventually increase your meditation time up to twenty minutes each day. Practice this consistently for one month, and then forever! You'll get into a groove if you "grow it" like most things in life. You are nourishing a new, holy habit. You will then have cultivated what Jesus describes as "the one thing necessary" (Lk. 10:42), where Mary, versus her busybody sister Martha, sat and enjoyed the presence of the Lord. That Gospel story can be viewed as a prototype and an inspiration for what we want to promote in meditation——stillness and focusing on God's presence!

Let us now go further into the "Three-R" process.

READ. Go over the text or review the image if it is a visual. It is important here to remember that the simpler the text, the better. It doesn't have to be involved or detailed or overladen with layers of meaning in which to become quagmired. If it is a text, limit it to a paragraph or shorter, Then, from either the text or image, extract the essence of the object. Find one thought or image to which your mind goes most easily or quickly. The faster you do this, the better. You don't want to be choosing many different objects during a meditation period, thus, spinning your inner wheels without a solid foundation, never settling in due to lack of selection and focus.

The object of meditation can either be, as we have said, textual or visual, explicitly religious (for example Christ himself, an angel, or saint) or something simple, such as a flower or animal or peaceful mountain scene that might remind you of the Creator's glory and power. This might be "religious" (implicitly so) in a different way to you than outright religious scenes. You can select an object of meditation from the Bible itself, or choose from the mysteries of the Rosary (twenty of them depict biblical stories) or, from the Stations of the Cross or a church's stained-glass windows. Once again, remember: simplicity!

While having emphasized the need for simplicity, there is another side to that coin—you want detail, fleshiness, specificity. Our minds do not do so well, especially for beginners of meditation, with blankness, abstraction, thinking of something when there's basically nothing to stimulate the thinking. For instance, to meditate on a cloud or, the sky or God or grace is difficult and sometimes nebulous. We usually need concrete, enfleshed details, depth, and color. We want that "Imax approach"—a flooding of the senses so that they are all interested, involved and engaged.

REFLECT. This step primarily concerns the intellect—your brain, by thinking, and, especially by your power of focusing. After reading or visualizing within (step one), now, in this second step (keeping in mind that the "steps" are subtle and not always sharply defined), stimulate curiosity about it, the object, and intellectualize, mindfully, forming simple, meaningful thoughts about it. What is the subject matter of the scene or thought read or reviewed? What do you see and sense and what, if any, action is taking place?

Here, you have two options and either one is valid. You can "brainstorm" or "free-associate." You may think many different but related thoughts about the object, emphasizing variety and spontaneity, or you may think deeply about one or two thoughts and focus on them. The point is to stimulate the intellect and then focus. That is the key: focusing on one thought, image, or action.

RESPOND. This is the main step, stimulating feeling, consolations, and heartfelt sensations about the object of meditation. The main components of this step include gratefulness, emotion-feeling, and resolution. In this step, we want to use our hearts (versus our heads) to have inner dialogues of feeling—conversations with God, or with self. We want to develop affection for the Lord, or his ways (such as exemplified in the life of a saint or in an aspect of holiness). Therefore, we stimulate and utilize our emotions and passions in response to the thinking process.

In this step, we also want to cultivate resolutions of how we will respond to the meditation and actualize change in our lives, versus just keeping it in our heads without following through.

A PRACTICAL EXAMPLE

Now, let's use the example of meditation on the Transfiguration of Jesus upon the mountain. Either choose a picture of our luminous Lord from the Transfiguration that portrays light, radiance, life, lightness, and/or read slowly Matthew 17:1-8:

> *After six days, Jesus took Peter, James, and John, his brother, and led them up a high mountain by themselves. And he was transfigured before them; his face shone like the sun and his clothes became white as light. And behold, Moses and Elijah appeared to them, conversing with him. Then Peter said to Jesus in reply, "Lord, it is good that we are here. If you wish, I will make three tents here, one for you, one for Moses, and one for Elijah."While he was still speaking, behold, a bright cloud cast a shadow over them, then from the cloud came a voice that said, "This is my beloved Son, with whom I am well pleased; listen to him." When the disciples heard this, they fell prostrate and were very much afraid. But Jesus came and touched them,*

saying, "Rise, and do not be afraid." And when the disciples raised their eyes, they saw no one else but Jesus alone.

After slowly reading the text or reviewing the image, construct the scene within your mind and internalize the divine sight—make it real, within.

Visualize Christ on the mountain and/or other figures in the scene. Use all your senses: sight, sound, touch, and even smell.

Reflect upon and think about the various persons and happenings of this sacred story. You could, for instance, focus on what St. Peter says, "It is good to be here" (Mt. 17:4). While the first step involved the basics of the scene, composing it sensually, this step involves depth, thinking, ruminating about the scene or main focus.

Next, reflect. Use your head—which obviously involves thinking. Basically, think a little about your main object of meditation, whether it be Christ himself or St. Peter or the luminous light radiating toward you. Not everyone can think great thoughts and gain insights, but everyone can harvest inspirations from a text such as this.

Respond to the text or image. Respond means heartfulness-feeling and is more important than reflection and thinking. If thinking is "Einsteinian," then responding is child-likeness; it means utilizing emotion, feeling and intuitional responsiveness in a simple and pure way. You may want to respond by thanking Jesus for his Divine Radiance. Let it seep in. Praise him and look forward to your own participation in his gracing you more in the future. Feel that goodness from Him (don't just think about it). Notice your heart grow and glow. Let your emotions flow from the reflection step, deepen them and allow them to transform you. We will cover this meditation more deeply in the next chapter as it is rich and vibrant for our spiritual lives!

OTHER TIPS ON MEDITATION

PLACE. We should, and can, pray and meditate anywhere, and yet we should cultivate a special space—a place for meditation that draws us into and protects and promotes regular meditation. Let's first consider the "pray anywhere" counsel. If you can't get to the chapel or your special spot of prayer, then don't let that stop or subterfuge you! Pray and meditate (as I have) in the car, at the playground, in an office cubicle or bedroom. I recall hearing from a busy mom who was a lay Carmelite that she was retreating to her bathroom! After developing your meditation life, this becomes basic common sense—you can pray anywhere, meditate "on your feet" if need be. You have an interior life; so, enable it wherever you find yourself, even in action!

As for the "sacred space" counsel, we shouldn't be so casual as to neglect our soul and a sacred space for meditation. We need the help and discipline of a place of consistency. If we're serious about exercising, we go to a gym; so, like Russian and Orthodox Christians, we could create a "red corners" in our homes—special, sacred places, perhaps with an altar, icon or candle, to inspire the soul into its spiritual center, a place of quiet and serenity that invites, attracts, "calls." Fashion in some way a simple, special place to which you can regularly retreat. The more explicit, the better—a room or corner of the home is best, but, once again, we all have to be realistic. Maybe, for you, it's the side of your bed with a decorated table nearby, or the corner sofa in a family room with religious pictures close by, or a comfy chair amidst a work room.

TIME. Here's Tip #1: Meditation is best in the morning and, better yet, in the morning *and* at nighttime—creating a "bookends" approach of constancy by this. You are thus cultivating rhythm and continuity. Early morning helps you "get out of the gate" well and stabilizes your day and evening recollection helps frame and end your day.

Tip #2: Meditate whenever you can. Perhaps it's a coffee or lunch break, or when the kids go to school, or they are with other families, or in between appointments. The important idea is to make a daily appointment time with your Lord and your inner soul. Remember, when you get out of the habit it's usually very difficult to get back into the "meditative groove," especially with the tenacious treadmill world in which we live!

POSTURE. Here, let's apply the Latin axiom, *conincidentum oppositorum,* or co-incidence of opposites. In this case, we'll describe the meditation posture as one of "noble-relaxation." Noble implies uprightness and firmness, an awareness pervading throughout the body, and relaxation denotes the absence of rigidity and tightness. Whether meditating in the car or church pew or office workspace, here are some essentials: Sit upright, feet on the floor, shoulders spread without slumping, head-neck-chin alert, facing forward without tightness or agitation or strain. Sometimes, kneeling is good for shortish periods. What you want to avoid in all postures, is being over-relaxed, falling asleep, becoming slothful and sluggish and, oppositely, any rigidity and discomfort.

There are many reasons for all these descriptors above that we won't go into but, suffice to say now, we Christians awaken and utilize the body as a temple of the Holy Spirit (1 Cor. 6:17), while also not idolizing certain physical positions as essential to salvation or enlightenment.

On a daily basis, establish an ongoing consistency in prayer and your time devoted to meditation as this is better than "spiritually splurging." Better to pray/meditate ten minutes a day, every day, for three weeks, than to pray one hour only once a week. Then, just as with anything else, as you take baby steps to build up a virtue or habit, increase your dedication and thus build up your time in meditation, focus, and concentration, to the point that it becomes second nature. In essence, you want to become like a paced marathon runner in for the long haul, versus the short-term spurts of a sprinter. Put another way: You are developing the prayerful habit of focused intimacy and an interior life.

MEDITATION AND PRAYER

FAITH FORMULA

There are other important elements of meditation we all need to embrace and, eventually master.

STILLNESS is physical. We all need to be still, in and throughout our bodies, at least, sometimes. Master the act of actually sitting still—after being wound up so much, you'll need to unwind. You need to do this—actually BE still—maybe not like the Buddha or a Hindu guru, in a contorted lotus position, but we do need basic relaxation and physical stillness for our meditative soul, interior life, and calming of the mind. Remember this general principle: the physical leads to the metaphysical. In other words, a calm body helps pacify the soul.

SILENCE means inner and outer quietude. Turn off the radio, TV, doorbell (if you still have one), switch off the computer, and whirring of various machines, especially when you are beginning meditation. You need all the external silence possible. Now, for interior silence, this is the more challenging type of silence to engender within the mind and soul. It's likely you will have the proverbial flywheel hamster-thoughts running within your mind and you might become frustrated because you are seemingly unable to easily turn off these internal operations and interminable thoughts of out-of-control mind. Fear not! Persevere, and the more you focus (concentrate on the object of meditation) you replace that mental static and gradually overcome it. Work through it, as virtually every meditator has needed to do this in the history of the world.

GRACE is God's life and helps to us. One of the main differences between Western Christian meditation and Eastern religions is that we rely upon grace (God's help) whereas in the East it's more about one's own work and effort minus God's assistance. That's definitely a generalization but we Christians should stress our reliance upon God. It's not all about us, our efforts and techniques, or gnostic wisdom we put together in the right building-block syndrome wherein we master enough to eventually "deliver God." (This is what Catholics and others decry when disapproving certain spiritual "techniques.") We need God himself and his helping grace because we are sinners, weak and wandering, through a mysterious path and nothing, no one but God, can help us.

FOCUS is self-disciplined concentration. Whereas vocal prayer ("oration") consists of many focus points, and is varied as a kaleidoscope of subjects, in meditation, there is one main focus or target-point. With so many today flailed by multi-tasking directions and an "always-wired" mentality, inner concentration can seem impossible. Many can't (or won't) sit still or quiet the precocious mind. Focus means a still mind and accumulative ability to zero in on a spiritual subject and concentrate, within.

EXPERIENCE is the ultimate goal. So, okay, read this book but then move on to actual meditation itself—interior focus and the quiet experience of God. Isn't that what so many are looking for today—not only God himself but simple ways to experience him? We have to practice and love sitting in stillness, silence and inner concentration to focus on God and his way of life provided for us. Nothing can replace this. So, *meditate*!

REASONS ... OR EXCUSES TO QUIT

St. Teresa of Avila describes meditation, and inspires us to use our mind and senses, by disallowing them from wandering and focusing upon one object of love. She writes in *The Way of Perfection*: "It is called recollection because the soul collects together all the faculties and enters within itself to be with God." Yes, recollection is so challenging today, and gathering all of our senses and powers within, but no one is going to do it for you and it will always be challenging; so, *if not now, when?*

Here are my A-B-C-D Reasons why people don't meditate or cultivate an interior life. (And, herein, lie some of our most important enemies for which we need to watch out!)

"A" is for Apathy. This is perhaps in all of us and it may be called the "inner slacker." It's as though there's someone inside, saying, "Don't try" or "Just give up" and, so we do—and then don't pray or practice stillness. We cave into or cultivate an "I-just-don't-care" attitude about our spiritual and interior lives. It becomes passé. After so many "cave-ins" or postponements, we consciously or unmindfully become apathetic. So, realize and resolve that your most important job, task, goal, vocation-calling today, is to be still, silent and communing with the Lord.

"B" is for busyness—most everyone claims they are always busy or in a "rat race." You've heard that or have said it, yourself. So, we perpetuate within ourselves, or to others, a self-fulfilling prophecy: "Busyness is the natural state of the world—and mine." We begin believing this ideological toxin and spreading it into others, thereby furthering this modern American myth. Yes, it's sometimes "easier" just to stay on the "treadmill" (or "rat race") and attach to externals such as job, possessions, activities, versus doing the hard work of the interior life that requires self-discipline and inner direction. Simplify your life and activities, accept slowness, contentment, a "new normal" of calmness—and you'll nurture the ability to be still and silent with the Lord more naturally.

"C" is for challenge. Mental prayer or cultivating an interior life might seem complex and foreign or alien to daily life. It's a challenge so we resist it or just don't do it. We take the path of least resistance. Just as you work through those meticulous foreign-language instructions on how to put together your plasma TV or coffeemaker, so you can also master the basics of the interior life, which aren't all that complex when you get down to it: be still, silent, focus, love God in meditation! The thing is we all need to persevere and overcome challenges in the interior lift.

"D" is for distractions. We all get them and sometimes they seem inevitable and/or overwhelming. Because we get so many, so often, even before we begin a formal time of meditation, we might resist the inner life. Put bluntly: at the least sign of trouble we give up or don't continue! Don't shoot yourself in the "spiritual foot" by listening to the ego say: "Last time you prayed, meditated, your mind wandered the whole time." Rather work through distractions and be at peace.

ASPIRATIONS

In the Catholic-Christian tradition, we have a beautiful discipline called, "aspirations," or, in the older parlance, "ejaculations." The East calls these short prayers "mantras." This is a marvelous way to carry your meditative, still, and silent prayer into the active realm when you need be busy and do things—as we all must do.

The word *aspire* means "to go upward," and ejaculation comes from the Latin root, "to hurl" (as like a javelin in Roman times). Thus, Christians "throw up a short prayer to God" when they can't pray longer prayers.

Such aspirations can be offered as meditative words, phrases, or short prayers, prayed repeatedly from our lips to focus our minds and hearts as we are doing some kind of activity, which does not allow "usual" prayer.

Perhaps the most famous aspiration is "The Jesus Prayer," based in part on Luke 18:13:

Lord Jesus Christ, only Son of God, have mercy on me, a sinner.

This aspiration is the subject of innumerable books, classic treatises, and spiritual commentary spanning centuries. The best

continue page 53 »

and simplest counsel out of all that wisdom is to simply say the prayerful phrases with meaning and heartfelt intention.

One of my favorite aspirations is:

O Sacrament most holy / O Sacrament Divine / All praise and all thanksgiving / Be every moment Thine.

After you memorize this aspiration, you may pray it in a singsong rhythm in the phrases marked above. It can become like all ejaculations—infectious, rhythmic, once you memorize it. And that is the point to give your whole being to God and/or, in my colloquial term, to "hijack" your brain and calm your soul in the rhythm of the prayer.

Other aspirations you may use include:

- "God, come to my assistance / Lord, hasten to help me" used in beginning the Liturgy of the Hours—the prayer of the Psalms.

- "My Lord and My God"—St. Thomas' exclamation about the risen Jesus in John 20:28.

- "Jesus, I trust in You!"—The Divine Mercy prayer and devotion.

- "Lord, I need you."

- "Lord Jesus, help me."

- "Lord Jesus, I need you, I love you, I trust you."

CHAPTER FOUR

Aspects of Prayer and Meditation

"It is good to be here"
(Mk. 17:4)
—St. Peter at the
Transfiguration of Jesus

Yes, "It is good to be here." Where? With God in prayer and adoration—anywhere, where we can be still and silent, to fully accept and visualize the Lord's radiating Love coming to us. In the Transfiguration story St. Peter and the Apostles left the world an experience of Christ's revelation of divinity on the mountaintop, and, in a way, so you can share this experience now, in the here and present moment of your life wherever that may be. Though we just covered this biblical text in the last chapter we return to it now as repetition is a foundational discipline in meditative life!

Notice that in the Transfiguration (which is a classic of meditation, especially in the East) the Apostles had to:

1. Leave behind,
2. Go up,
3. Encounter the Lord Jesus' radiance divine.

Let's now look at each of these elements that will help us develop an interior life and meditation.

LEAVE BEHIND. This means all practicing Christians have to depart from harmful or illegitimate people, places, and things, and get rid of any and all distractions and detriments before God. Perhaps, you are overly attached to the daily news or a hobby or a person or favorite drink. This might prevent you from time with God. Your ego struggles to detach, to "leave behind" some people or things at some level for something or someone better! So, *go*! Thus, you need to subtract anything along the way that distorts, keeps you behind, and loads you down and this will eventually bother you less and less in meditation.

GO, UP. This means going toward God! This does not mean you necessarily have to go away to a church (although, it might be helpful, if possible) or flee to a "desert" for God, but, perhaps, go to somewhere close and accessible in your home, in your workplace, or, even in your car or a nearby park, to make time for prayer and spiritual encounter. As long as it can be a routinely-accessible place, anything can be your cloister!

RECEIVE. You have to be capable of receiving God—versus being wearied, frazzled, or fazed. Be calm and peaceful. How receptive-absorbent are you? Can you receive God into your soul, or, are you too overloaded with thoughts, worries and errant desires? When I was at the oceanside one time with friends, one of them said, "This is so healing… just being at the beach." Why? The ocean and salt air and water and wind and sky and surroundings are vast, pervading and beautiful—a God-given "spiritual amalgamation" that medicates and calms us. So the grace of God can help us even more!

PRACTICAL APPLICATION

Read Matthew 17:1-8 and reflect on it or look at a painting or picture of the Transfiguration.

> *After six days Jesus took Peter, James, and John his brother, and led them up a high mountain by themselves. And he was transfigured before them; his face shone like the sun and his clothes became white as light. And behold, Moses and Elijah appeared to them, conversing with him. Then Peter said to Jesus in reply, "Lord, it is good that we are here. If you wish, I will make three tents here, one for you, one for Moses, and one for Elijah." While he was still speaking, behold, a bright cloud cast a shadow over them, then from the cloud came a voice that said, "This is my beloved Son, with whom I am well pleased; listen to him." When the disciples heard this, they fell prostrate and were very much afraid. But Jesus came and touched them, saying, "Rise, and do not be afraid." And when the disciples raised their eyes, they saw no one else but Jesus alone.*

Think about how Jesus went away and up to a mountain. Visualize (picture) within Christ in his glory and radiant splendor. Use all your senses to compose the scene with Christ in the middle of the mountaintop and apostles nearby him with a wearied world far below.

Now *reflect*. This means use your head (intellect) and ponder the scene in the "inner Imax-theater" of your mind. Think about Christ there, a tall, ruddy, handsome man standing and emitting translucent, ethereal, piercing Light, while you are riveted right where you are and you feel warm, aglow, one with his Light. The Light is pulsing into you and you are elevated, made light-airy, and (hopefully) affixed to him now. He is obviously, metaphysically different, God, yet approachable, embracing you. Time is still, non-existent. You are free and exultant.

Respond. Thank him. Use your heart, sentiments, emotions, feelings to attach to Christ. "It is good to be here," you might feel and say with St. Peter. You are thankful, tranquil. Express all this to Jesus, the Lord, who shared with the Apostles (and you) his divinity and healing grace. Let your feelings-response be a "spiritual glue" that affixes you to him, in solidarity of soul, just as when you are with a friend and want to be with him/her forever, more deeply. You want more of Jesus, to be closer to him and desire that these desires, through this meditation of sentiments and emotions, may last and enmesh you more to him.

The purpose of meditation, as we have stressed, is to develop true discipleship, deeper Christian love and the habit of being, interiorly and, eventually, holistically, with God, 24/7.

Our prayer lives can be like that. By developing it into a holy habit, our closeness to God becomes more real and permanent. By this "spiritual subtraction and addition"—letting go, stripping away to make way for the "and" of freely receiving his Divinity—as exemplified through the Transfiguration journey and encounter, we disciples develop our interior lives more firmly and love him, more!

Think. When you go to a retreat or on a vacation and you arrive at that place apart and your "soul breathes" because it is emptying out toxins and past troubles and is resting in a vivid and healing emptiness, and as you are more at peace, emptied, you can be filled with God speaking to you and infusing his grace within you. Jesus wants you to make this journey, daily, in meditation—the transfiguration of soul awaits.

MORE PRAYER BASICS

As we have learned, meditation is a simple form of prayer to unite the soul to God, primarily through silence, focus, and stillness. Remember the story we read about Jesus' visit to Martha and Mary, and Christ's words to the frenzied hostess: "The Lord said to her in reply, 'Martha, Martha, you are anxious and worried about many things. There is need of only one thing. Mary has chosen the better part and it will not be taken from her'" (Lk. 10: 41-42). Notice the spiritual importance of what is in this text: choosing focused stillness and deepened love that will not be taken from Mary.

Within-ness. This is the ability to detach from the outside world and go within and be focused and still. Thus, we can liken the mind and soul as to an "internal internet library," a wealth of information and images to instantly feed upon and think about, for our interior life—if we can consciously and continuously go within and not be distracted by the outside world.

We use the term meditation sometimes in the sense of "spiritual focusing" as contrasted with contemplation, which is "spiritual resting." Meditation *focuses* and contemplation *rests*. They are separate but related spiritual disciplines, and meditation is the foundation of contemplation, as we have stated. While it is classically understood that not all are called to contemplation (it is a rare gift from God and takes much discipline, simplicity, and heroic-pure love), we are all called to mental prayer, to meditation—inward focus. This is reachable for all.

Prayer, classically understood, as St. John Damascene said, is the "raising of mind and heart to God." In prayer we use our minds (thoughts) and also our hearts (feelings) to commune with God, just as we use mind and heart, in daily life, in relationship with others.

PRACTICES

An important point: repetition with heart and keeping focused upon our spiritual object of consideration is all-important. That takes a skillful balance of mindfulness to pray prayers through thick and thin, while also intending the spiritual words we say or pray. We will, in the beginning when trying this form of prayer, either end up in babble—good at repetition but not good at intention and depth, or else we will mire into skittishness—excel in depth or meaning but losing rhythm and repetition.

Usually, when I go into a church, I have a normal repertoire of prayer to begin, because I know from past experience, of being so skittish and fragmented by daily life, and barely praying or being mindful in that chapel visit, I can sometimes walk out from the church and ask myself—"Did I really talk to Jesus—really meet him?" So I've developed a couple of prayers I always say, pray, slowly, to make sure that intimate contact is made and thereby deepen my prayer, and get my meditation started in a proper, personal way.

We talked earlier about aspiration-prayer, so, here's a short prayer I suggest to you, which you can adapt especially for church visits:

> *Lord, Jesus Christ, I know You are truly present, Body and Blood, Soul and Divinity in the Blessed Sacrament of the Eucharist. May Your eucharistic Body lift up my body. May your Divinity refresh my humanity. Amen.*

This reminds me, helps me be mindful, that Jesus is really there in church, before me—eucharistically present; that He is God and man, divine and human; and that He can grace and re-create me. This reminds me to mindfully make conscious contact with Him. And that he is a person, a divine person who wants and deserves heart-to-heart communion versus rote babble words. This prayer, when prayed mindfully, slowly (versus racing through it) helps me connect with him, realize his Divine Presence before, around me, and get my prayer off to a good start.

When meditating, we need some of these elements in order to foster an interior life: good beginnings and intentions, personal involvement of both self (fully conscious of what we are doing) and of course God, whom we acknowledge in need of his grace and supernatural grace and involvement. Upshot: we are not just "going through the motions" in zombie-like fashion; rather depth and focus are always important elements of meditation.

Another helpful prayer is: *Lord Jesus, I need you, I love you, I trust you.*

Basically, this says it all. It expresses our need, our surrender to him, Christ, our affection for him. We abandon and entrust ourselves to God. We need to both say it and mean it. Perhaps you can use this prayer as a beginning to your meditation period—with your heart.

I've learned that while traveling, which I do a lot in the car, I can't always be in church praying my holy hour (before Jesus in the Blessed Sacrament-Eucharist in the tabernacle). So, along the way, as I am driving, I use the aspiration I mentioned earlier: "O Sacrament most holy, O Sacrament Divine, All praise and all thanksgiving: Be every moment Thine!"

This is a traditional prayer in Mass and in eucharistic devotion—a song, really, which helps when you sing it, within, creating a soothing and melodic aspiration which eventually "repeats itself within" the more you pray it mindfully—which is one more "sticking point" to help you keep the rhythmic depth.

While driving, sometimes during late nights, before arriving back in my church (where I usually make my holy hour—prayer time before Jesus in the Eucharist), I would begin this prayer-aspiration and become relaxed, focused, so much so that when I did finally arrive at the Church, I realized only later, after a few minutes, that I was still repeating the aspiration within, even though I was finally there before Christ Our Lord! I had developed rhythmic depth and still not caused an accident on the road!

You can develop this interior devotion and prayer of the heart with these small spiritual surges and aspirations that will carry you through the day in prayer!

Here are some recommendations for you: choose one aspiration to be recited for a whole week, versus picking a different aspiration every day. This consistency will help you learn and meld it, the aspiration, into your soul. When you wake up in the morning, it hopefully will become a natural prayer-phrase that you immediately say, as well as repeating doing this at other times during the day, increasing the spontaneity of prayer and familiarity with the aspiration.

TYPES OF PRAYER

Now, let's do a brief review of the various types of prayer that we should all pray daily, along with and in meditation.

ACTS...

The acronym ACTS is probably one of the most famous spiritual ones in the world for prayer. Perhaps you know it, have used it or maybe would like to learn it...

A = Adoration means worship of God, our most important and first act of religion. We should love him with all our hearts: If we miss this, then we are erring in our faith, prayer, and spiritual lives. Worship of God comes first.

C = Contrition means being sorry for our sins, yes, even in this age of self-perfection and pride. Tell Our Lord, in prayer, your defects, express remorse, and seek mercy.

T = Thanksgiving, being grateful is always great and also makes us happier. Daily, think of the many ways God has blessed you and thereby "stretch your heart" in gratefulness.

S = Supplication involves praying for others, intercession. Think of all the people and events you can pray for and do it!

Since being holistic is an in-thing these days, the ACTS acronym prayer-prescription is one way to be vogue in your spiritual life by utilizing all these forms of prayer through your meditation. For instance, on one day, you can emphasize meditation on the cross of Jesus (visualize it, read about the Passion in the Gospels) and on another day think about his mercy and also express your sorrow and contrition. Another day you can emphasize adoration as you, perhaps, rejoice in his Resurrection appearances, praying like St. Thomas, "my Lord and my God" (Jn. 20:26).

PRAYER AND BREATHING

Remember I said I would further explain the title *Thirty-three Breaths*? So: Jesus lived thirty-three years on earth and in honor of his Incarnation-Enfleshment, when praying, I have learned to take thirty-three deep, long, rhythmic in-and out-breaths, counting slowly, peacefully, and thus creating a little meditation period which is manageable and, hopefully, mystical. During this time you may be thinking of his birth, his preaching or walking on water, simply and slowly, and pray through your breath and calm the mind and still the thoughts in you, which may be turbulent or tired, and receive Jesus' Spirit!

You always have time for this, breathing thirty-three times, slowly in and out. Everyone can do this, perhaps multiple times a day. This prayer-practice helps me daily: slowly, rhythmically counting the breath—thirty-three times in a brief-but generous and doable period of meditation. I practice it when I am exasperated or beginning or concluding a holy hour in church (meditation-time before the Eucharist), or sitting in the car at a traffic light or stop sign, or while waiting for someone, or just waking up in the morning. This prayer is flexible and convenient; you can do it anytime, anywhere and do the count of thirty-three times on your fingers and thereby free the mind and heart to focus on the content of your prayer. It's transportable and transposable and can be done anywhere and applied in so many ways.

Now let's consider how we can link our breathing to God since He created us and, originally, Adam, by bestowing his Divine Breath into all of us. First, here are some biblical passages related to the breath that illustrate the importance of holistic-breathing meditation; that it's not just for "spiritual masters" or new-agers or yoga experts.

- Genesis 2:7—"Then the Lord God formed man of dust from the ground, and breathed into his nostrils the breath of life, and man became a living being."

- Genesis 6:17, 7:15, and 7:22—The "breath of life" is mentioned in these passages as part of the constitution, or make-up, of man and creation.

- Job 27:3—"All the while my breath is in me, and the spirit of God is in my nostrils."

- Job 33:4—"For the spirit of God made me, the breath of the Almighty keeps me alive."

- John 20:22—"And when he (Jesus in His resurrection) had said this, he breathed on them and said to them, 'Receive the holy Spirit.'"

- 1 Corinthians 3:16—St. Paul asks: "Do you not know you are the temple of God, and that the Spirit [Breath] of God dwells in you?"

- 2 Timothy 3:16—"All Scripture is God-breathed and is useful for teaching, rebuking, correcting and training in righteousness." (This is the New International Version. The Greek word, according to the website Bible Hub, is theópneustos, which literally means "God-breathed," likely a term coined by Paul.)

Breathing is part of normal and daily life and our relationship with God because, since Adam, we have been created by God's divine breath. Since the time of Pentecost (see: Acts ch. 1) the Holy Spirit dwells in us personally, and transforms us. So, it is no mistake—or sin—that when Eastern Christians or others meditate on and with the breath, this is a biblical/metaphysical process and discipline, not a mechanical technique to "produce God" or a mind-state of selfish egoism.

Just why is this so important for a Catholic-Christian? Breathing is the most important and intimate thing we do. It can be a mode of consistency in our prayer. Breathing is our most integral and important function. Without breath we would die in a few minutes. Simply think about it: we all have to do it, and need to do it: breathe! So, why not "spiritually harness" it? Why not use it more explicitly in our prayer, as Jesus used his divine breath to awaken the disciples in his Resurrection? The breath can assist us internally (guiding our focus) or externally, by following it physically.

Breathe—consciously. Slow and mindfully. Breathing can make us peaceful or panicked; the choice is ours. And didn't your mom say something like this when you were growing up and came home upset? As in: "Johnny (or Jean), calm down, stop, slow down, take some deep breaths and tell me again just what happened. ..." She (nor anyone else) ever said, "Breathe real short breaths and start panting!"

While we cannot ever make breathing a "spiritual technique"— something to "produce God" or "engineer enlightenment"—we can adapt to our "body language"—how God designed our body's mechanics—and even in the way God in the past has awakened man (see biblical citations above). We should call this a discipline or a method—a physical-mental-spiritual action that assists us in praying, such as physically kneeling while praying at Mass, saying the words of a Psalm out loud, using a hymnal to sing a song, or focusing on a text of devotional meditation or envisioning

BREATHING, FREEING, SEIZING

When I was on vacation one time years ago, this following meditation came to me. It originated from a text of the Liturgy of Hours (the prayer book of priests and professed religious) and became subject matter for silent reflection later in Mass time—and later in life. The meditation is: *Breathing/Freeing/Seizing ...*

BREATHING is the most basic thing we do in life and the simplest and "nearest" thing to utilize. Everyone must breathe and when we are mindful in meditation, we need go nowhere or to anyone else since we always have our breathing with us. You don't have to be creative or look around for a meditation—you always have your breath. When I breathe mindfully, slowly, rhythmically, I can be more in touch with God as all my body and senses calm and gather within God's providence and presence.

FREEING means we need to be liberated and unchained from sin to love God, to be present to him and detach to fully give ourselves to him to meditate. Remember, Jesus came to free us from sins (Lk. 19:10—"to seek and save what was lost"). The name "Jesus," from the Hebraic *Jeshua* means "He will save his people from their sins" (see Mt. 1:21). Thus, Jesus is our "Savior," our emancipator, the one who rescues us from any kind of bondage or addictions or attachments. He unknots the ancient bond with which the serpent-Satan tied us all in the Garden of Eden (Gn. 3:1-7).

Another image and reference point for "freeing" is to visualize Lazarus coming out of the tomb, after being dead for days, and Christ's command, "untie him" (Jn. 11:44); or, imagine Peter in chains in prison and being liberated (Acts 5:19).

Remember, we need freedom from outright sins or enslavements. We can become allured (a little amount of unhealthy connection) or attached (larger amount of unhealthy relationship) or even addicted,

continue page 67 »

the worst, most dangerous bondage, whereby we "need" the thing or experience and are enslaved to it. Given all this, we need to be liberated to love God truly and to rest in his Divine Presence in meditation.

SEIZING basically means union with God. Our purpose in life and within meditation is to form a union with God or, more properly, him coming and embracing us through his grace to our waiting and freed souls. Everything else is secondary.

For the first word in our prayer-aspiration, "breathing," I thought of three images or visualizations, which may help you to "concretize" this meditation:

1. God breathing into Adam, who was previously the clay of the earth, to give him life (Gn. 2: 7).

2. God breathing into the dry bones of Israel (Ez. 37:1f).

3. Jesus breathing into the disciples at the Resurrection (Jn. 20:22).

Read these passages and while praying/meditating, envision an image of one of them, and "bond" with it. Internalize this process. Make it your own. Simply, slowly, breathe—calmly, with awareness on your conscious breathing in and out.

In this particular meditation, you can also visualize your breath going into the eucharistic tabernacle in church where Jesus dwells in his True Presence. Like a hovering cloud commingling with the mountain rock in Bible images, so your breath can go into the tabernacle, to commingle with Jesus in the holy Bread, and seize, grasp him. Your breath-spirit is now enclosed with him.

Breathing ... Freeing ... Seizing.

an icon in church. All of these physical-spiritual methods are like utilizing the breath as an "accessory." These are methods that are ancient practices of our spirituality that we are advised by the Church to utilize.

Learn, through your prayer, to slow your breath, calm yourself, and follow your breath into deeper concentration and focused meditation.

THE SOUL AND PRAYER DIFFICULTIES

We all have troubles in prayer, and that includes the most mystic of saints. When describing their prayer lives, many saints spoke of darkness or dark nights or difficult life-passages. Realize that you will likely go through them too! We all will have some darkness or distractions, some kinds of problems in focusing, meditating, and keeping our attention on God or our process of prayer. However, never tire of prayer or give up. Persevere. We've already discussed some challenges in our prayer life, so let's now uncover some more of these common problems of prayer and consider suggested solutions:

DARK NIGHTS

Everyone wants to deny or avoid this inevitable stage of the spiritual life. But we're all going to go through some troubles in our prayer lives and, maybe even some "purgatories" and more. Just like Jesus, we need to imitate him as He went through darkness and desolation—on the Cross and in the Garden of Gethsemane. If we are prepared for the darkness, we will not turn away from our holy habit of meditation, but, rather, persevere.

In an important book (and Time Magazine cover story for April 17, 2014), *Learning to Walk in the Dark*, author and preacher Barbara Brown Taylor confronted the modern-Pollyanna-ish desire for continual "religious desserts" and "saccharine spirituality" instead of the Cross or the sandpapery approach of the saints who embraced Christ's way of divine darkness in order to detach from all that is not God. Darkness can be a unique and counter-intuitive gift from God, useful and purifying and, part of his beguiling plan. Using darkness as a metaphor, as many Christian spiritual writers do, Taylor writes: "I have learned through things in the dark that I could never have learned in the light, things that saved my life over and over again, so that there is only one logical conclusion: I need darkness as much as I need light."

Part of following Jesus in our prayer lives is what is sometimes called the "desert experience"—as when the Israelites spent forty years there. after the Exodus liberation John the Baptist lived there and Jesus spent forty days and nights in the desert. So we, too, must go there and learn from it!

The stages of the spiritual life include purification. This is when the "gloves come off" and God shows us our muckiness—our personal suffering and failures, sins and effects of sin, attachments we have and their deleterious effects upon us, distractions and inability to focus on prayer, our lust and anger or envy. We need to see this so as to purify it all to become fully capable of receiving God himself.

We must distinguish what is from the Devil and what is from us. What is legitimately "welling up" within, that we note precisely because we are still and silent, and what are bad spirits doing to us? If the inner struggles are "legitimate" (and not torments of bad spirits), we need to reconcile with them, work through them, and learn how this darkness, like Israel's exile and Babylon's persecution of them taught them their culpability and frailty and Yahweh's majesty and mercy upon all of us. Part of this thinking about our sins, faults, and defects, attachments is not to go into endless psychobabble and selfish preoccupation, but rather to enter into true transparency with God's grace liberating us.

Since we are growing in love and the discipline of stillness, we can see and detect more through our prayer and we thus gain what is called a "sensitive conscience"—becoming able to pick out more "spiritual dust" and "debris" that adversely affects the life of the soul.

Remember, we will have darkness in our prayer lives, sometimes long or short, maybe even repetitive (periods when it comes and goes and returns again), and we thus need to strive and struggle through these times—persevere, not suppress them—and learn and move on, having been freed by the "dark spiritual process."

The saints understood that God prunes us like the vine-grower prunes the vines (see Jn. 15:1-8) and that any sane soul will have to undergo much purification, if not suffering, so as to grow in spiritual perfection. Purification is needed. When we pray more and more, we realize more and more how imperfect we are, and oppositely, how pure and sovereign God is and the distinct difference between us. Hopefully, we want to clean up our messiness and we can do this through God's purifying darkness and liberation of the soul.

Everyone experiences dark nights—either consciously or not. This is a path of purification to higher spiritual life. When these nights or darkness or purification come, we should both be at least a little prepared but also persevering and ready to keep on keeping on. In your meditative life, you will have darkness and trials: Persevere! Never give up!

Sometimes in this beguiling purification process, perhaps you will have doubts about God and the darkness of your own soul. This can involve your intellect and faith and either hound or assist you in both your prayer and active life. Will you persevere as the saints have? Desolation and dryness are part of the spiritual life. Or, maybe you will have a lack of willpower and need to purify or necessarily work through some seeds within you of sloth and torpor. Or maybe you are approaching despair. But, fear not. God is cleansing us, as long as we are willing to undergo this purificatory process.

Some other counsel-reminders on this subject include:
- "Work with the darkness"
- Be patient
- Don't panic
- Don't misjudge
- Ask for some spiritual help from someone with experience

ASPECTS OF PRAYER AND MEDITATION

DISTRACTIONS

Why do we have so many distractions? There are many reasons.

- We receive certain traits of negativity from our parents' DNA and are subject to a certain amount of past events and patterns affecting us as we try to sit in church in silence. While this is true, always remember: we are not total victims. We have free will to make different conscious choices today and in prayer.

- All kinds of things during daily life affect us, from blaring TVs and radios to arguing workmates and neighborhood noises to an instant gratification culture, which titillates the mind with iPhone-texting-constant communication. Media proliferation affects us more than we can know.

- We're sometimes not disciplined enough to handle the thousands of negative thoughts a day that arise in our minds and so we simply succumb, give in, are trammeled—and this breeds more distraction.

- "Disposition to anarchy"—since we are fallen beings as an effect of original sin, the mind is darkened, unharmonious, and along with this is the adverse imbalance of body and soul. So, within, we have a "secret saboteur" of inner stillness and propensity toward anarchy and away from order, goodness and calm, especially within the restless mind.

- Comfortability with laxity. We don't want to "ramp it up" or improve in meditation. We accept our averageness and don't wish to work on cultivating good thoughts or focusing or emptying out the bad stuff.

- Like Adam and Eve, we are sometimes attracted to wrongful, bad things, including harmful thoughts. We have a part of ourselves we may term as "the dark side" and, after all, it is sometimes more comfortable or easy to think or do what is wrong, bad, than to think or do what is right and difficult.

FIGHT OR FLIGHT

Consider the following as solvents to those enemies of stillness and silence. When distractions/diversions appear in prayer or meditation, fight or flight can help.

FIGHT means tenacity and "mental grit," fighting off a distraction and using willpower, energy against it and, oppositely, to call on the Lord very directly, or repeat aloud or inwardly, your meditative word (or to vividly re-present your visualization again if that is appropriate). This involves both a going away from the distraction and coming toward the object of meditation. The more focused you become on the object, by returning directly to your text or icon or visualization, the better.

FLIGHT involves what we may call a "roll with the punches" or distractions versus the "fight" approach. A common spiritual saying from the Christian East advises to "look over the shoulder of the distraction, to the Lord," who is far taller and more attractive than this current distraction or persistent problem you have. So, go beyond/over/around the distraction and "Go with the flow" or channel the distraction and "turn it into good." For instance, let's say you go off-track and begin thinking in meditation of an attractive nature scene (or lady or gentleman), you saw during the day. Now see that distraction as an allowance of the Lord, a kind of "spiritual mirror" bouncing your awareness from delighting in that distraction or person or scene to "flight" and rather bouncing up to God, who is the creator of all and thus away from the object that previously captivated you. You can then return to your main object of meditation in peacefulness.

Amidst all this, the most important point regarding distractions is

ASPECTS OF PRAYER AND MEDITATION

placing your awareness—your "mind-focus"—upon the object again and again, to rest there and so become comfortable and still in that object. This means the repetitive, simple-but-delicate process of laser-beam focusing upon your object. This is one of the hardest things you will ever do, accomplish, but one of the best and most usable as it will be applicable to other activities in life.

Regarding inner focus and distractions, you should know there is no "silver bullet" solution to this—whether you're looking for an answer from a priest-friend or the sacred Himalayas, or some mystic—that can solve your enervation. You must focus and choose concentration yourself! Therefore, recall and practice the classic holy habit of re-focusing, and the wise admonition "Master the passions or they will master you."

Long story short: the attraction should win out over the distraction. The attraction is our meditative thought or subject matter, or image or word and the re-focusing upon it. The distraction you have can be anything from job troubles to a laundry list of to-do things to tiny dust particle problems to the stock market rise or fall. Whatever strategy you use to go from distraction to attraction is okay. Just remember the attraction should overwhelm or gradually win out over the distraction.

OUR SOUL'S POWERS

The powers of the soul, the will, memory and intellect, all have a role in our meditation and mental prayer, as well, of course, as affecting all parts of our lives. This may seem obvious but let's recall what these faculties (sometimes called "powers" or "operations") all do within the soul and how they affect our meditation. The intellect thinks, the will chooses (thoughts or actions), and the memory produces or recalls images, thoughts within. This last faculty is sometimes called in classic parlance, "the phantasy."

Now, regarding meditation specifically, we need to think the right thoughts (not random or bad thoughts) and, in particular, focus on the object of meditation. The intellect must feed upon thoughts, fed to it by the memory (which is like a mental storehouse), and the will must choose what is right and proper to ponder. This is a synthetic process of many parts and stages, all doing one thing, united.

Obviously, we sometimes either choose thoughts that are wrong or do not choose any particular thoughts at all as we become passive or subject to daydreaming or "overrun" by the past, bad-habit thoughts (such as lust or anger) which we've failed to vanquish. Either way, we need more discipline from the will as well as old habits. This comes, as we've said, by choosing, strong-willed and wisely, in each moment, the right thought, one thought at a time. This may seem boring or lame, but it is, in fact, one of the most important things in the world as we "become" our choices of thinking. And for meditation or an interior life, one of the worst things is caving into random thoughts. Here is where the soul and meditator must be united—all three powers of the soul—memory, intellect and will all teaming up, harmonious in pursuit of being still and considering the object of meditation, "the one thing necessary."

We must train these powers of the soul as if they were stallions leading a chariot, capable of much good or bad, depending upon the charioteer (remember the movie and famous wild chariot scene of the classic 1959 movie *Ben Hur*?). Do not become passive to these "stallion soul powers" as they can lead almost anywhere. Like a wise and strong charioteer, guide them so that you are at peace and composed on the right path in your meditation.

> *"Watch your thoughts, they become words; watch your words, they become actions; watch your actions, they become habits; watch your habits, they become character; watch your character; for it becomes your destiny." — Frank Outlaw*

HE
BREATHES
ME...

HE is God. He is my source, I am his creation.

BREATHES is, as in Genesis chapters 1 and 2, God breathing into Adam, the first man and me. God is our life-breath. His breath lifts and in-spires your body and soul.

ME is yourself, in this meditation, your awareness applied, and, in general, your whole life. God is literally breathing you and keeping you in existence.

Breathe in and out very slowly, rhythmically, and repeat these words above, in and through your relaxed-rhythmic breaths.

Let's apply this aspiration-meditation another way.

VISUALIZE (picture within) God breathing into you, the Holy Spirit coming into your mouth, nose or body. Or, you may visualize your daily life, on the go, and God breathing you into your action, events and daily life.

THINK (about) the fact He is God and divinizes you by his very nature of giving, bestowing, uniting himself to you and, also, empowering you in daily activities.

THANK him for "fueling" you, becoming part of you and empowering your life and activities. Let his breath go into your heart and enlarge it, change and stimulate it with good feelings.

CHAPTER FIVE

EXAMPLES OF MEDITATION

Before we delve into examples of meditation in this chapter, let us review why we teach meditation and what is unique about it.

If I had just thirty seconds to tell a nervous person next to me what the heart of meditation is, I would boil it down to five words: interiority, sustain, focus, unitive, composure.

In what way are these words relative to meditation?

INTERIOR: Meditation is going into, embracing within-ness, and entering the internal theater of mind and heart to converse with God.

Jesus points to this interiority as we've stressed elsewhere: "Go into your inner room and pray to your Father in secret" (Mt 6:6).

SUSTAIN: Deep meditation requires lingering-leisure time, not just for a minute or three, but ten or more. You want to embed within or have God impress graces upon you and, essentially, this God-giving process takes time especially with all the tasks you have and the speeding events around you do each day. Like Georgia O'Keefe, the famous American southwest landscape painter, said, "Friendships take time." And so does meditation!

FOCUS: Meditation is not a "salad bar spirituality" or pick-anything-you-want approach to prayer. Rather, meditation is pointed-concentration upon one image or a word or idea within your mind and heart, in a sustained measure. You must stay with the object, circling around and thinking upon it, versus the mind fluttering around many objects or pursuits.

UNITIVE: This means a "deep encounter," the intercourse of two parties: God and soul. Meditation is a binding process, a merger, as we described earlier, a "spiritual gluing together" of God and human nature.

COMPOSURE: Being still and quiet, together as one component involves calmness and integration. In meditation, we are practically peaceful, prayerful, not being a treadmill-devotee of motion or multiplicity, tension or constant dizzied consumption.

Meditation involves these five elements, and over time we must deeply integrate them into our lives of prayer and discipleship on a regular basis so that meditation becomes a desired, natural state.

SABBATH AND SERENITY

"...a Sabbath rest still remains for the people of God. And whoever enters into God's rest, rests from his own works as God did from his. Therefore, let us strive to enter into that rest, so that no one may fall after the same example of disobedience. Strive to enter into that rest" (Heb 4:9-11).

One Sunday a couple of years ago, I was slowly learning how "to Sabbath." Notice the description "to Sabbath." We can use this word and reality, Sabbath, as a verb—as in to "do Sabbath." (Pardon the paradox: doing and Sabbath seem to be opposites!) Anyway, this particular Sabbath, I was trying to simply do nothing, surrender to the late summer air and emptiness and Sunday simplicity— "Sabbath-ness." But there was part of me, my Italian-ness, or inner manliness I guess, which didn't want to Sabbath, as I wanted to keep on keeping on. So I did some reading, took a small walk, read some more, enjoyed some soup, sat on the porch and enjoyed looking out into the vast western skies, and kind of planned what I could do the rest of the day and, even wondered who I might visit later for dinner.

I eventually "caved," in a good way, and decided to enter into my completely empty Sunday environs, church, and rectory, all by myself, without executing any events or doing anything. I gradually gave in—"Sabbathed." It wasn't exactly comfortable at first, but became so as I acquiesced to God's gift to me—and all of us– and let go of my own busy plans or what I thought should happen.

Isn't that what we mean when we say "unwind"? Let go, unspin from the entire wound-up activities and thinking of a hectic life and embrace the present moment?

All this transpired after plotting in the morning (and the night before) various activities I could do to mitigate against that unproductive, guilty feeling of leisure. Growing up, I was always surrounded by people and activities in my big Italian family and so

continue page 80 »

being still or alone was now like a kind of death to me. That "plotting" I was doing on that slow Sabbath was kind of like putting my finger in the dike of aimlessness and an engulfing emptiness, and staving them off. That particular Sunday, I had countless options, but none of them confirmed. However, on that unique Sunday, I relented to my "inner guru"—and God—and didn't cave into activation and nervous busy-body-ism, but got into Sabbath de-activation. It was probably grace, not I. I actually thought of a parishioner who, in the past, had said that what we all need to do is slow down in life. This parishioner also stressed the importance of spending time with family on the Sabbath. Eventually, I realized that it's fine to just do nothing, be by myself, alone, and actually shut down totally, and physically be still, rest, simplify. It takes time.

Deep down, I was originally uncomfortable with nothing to do on the Sabbath. Okay, we all, to a greater or lesser extent, have that "spiritual saboteur" of peace and rest, even though we constantly complain about how busy we are and how little time we have. So, to come full-circle in this discussion, to "do the Sabbath" means living counter intuitively. We must undo things we've learned throughout our lifetimes and undo things within us—basically to undo ourselves!

"AS OUTSIDE, SO INSIDE"

The way you are on the inside of yourself may be far from how you are on the outside. So now, slow down, now. *Stop!* Part of meditation also occurs when you're not meditating. Your active life defines your interior life. This is or should be done precisely by not living a rat race and not stressing out that you don't have anything to stress about! Realize that we have many internal "spiritual saboteurs" that booby-trap us and make us remain overly active because we sometimes fear stillness and silence. Both stillness and silence are needed. One leads to and complements the other.

"Strive to rest"

Now, let's meditate upon this paradox based upon the book of Hebrews, 4:11. Simply sit in silence and think. For instance, sometimes you have to really work hard to get away for vacation, a day off, or a retreat. Sometimes you have to scurry for this or that, and hurry up to slow down, to stop, but it's so worth it. Imagine a racehorse out of the starting gates straining toward the finish line and then, quickly, slowing down, easing, and becoming tranquil. See within your mind your own soul stretching out of bondage (the horse's starting gate) and eventually toward God himself, true rest, being and tranquility, and: the (inner) horse in peace.

Or see yourself scurrying out of the office on a Friday afternoon, getting all your paperwork and calls done to reach that 5 p.m. "deadline"; all the frenzy of flying papers and computer whirring you, but, you have the image of sitting on the back deck of home, Friday night, when you can enjoy some rest, a cool drink, and your family's company. You made it.

Now, image yourself scurrying through all your work, or household chores, to now go to your corner room, or a far-off place to pray the Bible or meditate upon your favorite spiritual book. So, "Strive to rest."

Perhaps, these are some images to ruminate over this paradox of "strive to rest." Paradox, which we are emphasizing here, means something beyond our mental grasp; a phenomenon that transcends our usual, mundane understanding. Thinking about this enigma of faith will stretch our brains and reason and, while our meditation may not deliver a final a black-and-white answer or a clear-cut statement, our "resolution" may be a kind of question to be lived and mystery to embrace and enter into.

We don't typically think of "striving to rest" in normal, everyday life. However, prayer and meditation are like that: we may not have or readily understand all the "answers" of an enigma from our spiritual lives, but, once we enter into the paradox more consistently we will have more acceptance and peace to deal with various problems and tasks of life that we do encounter because we have learned to sit better and be still; "rest," as it were, in and through the clouds and fog of our world. Let us now enter more deeply into meditation with the examples below by actually practicing the "strive to rest" in daily life.

PRACTICES OF THE INNER LIFE

Following is a series of meditative reflections you may practice and that may help you cultivate an interior life in various ways. Some of these meditations will emphasize *lectio divina*, others will be visualization-oriented meditations, and further ones will be aspirations. All the variety of these meditations is to provide you with not only actual meditation content but also the various disciplines, accents, and aspects of meditation, which only come while meditating and praying to God. So, here are some initial illustrations for you to begin:

"Are you taking your 'meds'?" You may hear this question more frequently these days as more and more are sick and taking prescription medications—meds. However, in a way, shouldn't everyone be on the "prescription meds" of meditation and prayer? We need, through the medicine of meditation, deeper union with God, peace, mindfulness and serenity and an interior life!

As you know, the three most basic needs in life (that is, besides TV, junk food, and shopping—joke!) are air, water, and food. Without these, we die. Without air for even a few minutes, we're dead; without water for a few days, we're gone; without food, we last only a few weeks. In essence, we need food, air, and water, before and during anything else—they are the essentials of life, literally.

God fulfills these essential demands, in Jesus Christ, through concrete and spiritual ways. Thus, we can meditate in the following manner based on those facts:

AIR: John ch. 20, The Resurrected Jesus, breathing out into the Apostles.

WATER: John ch. 8, the woman at the well, thirsting for God.

FOOD: John ch. 6, The Eucharistic Discourse, God feeds us.

AIR

"And when he had said this, he breathed on them
and said to them, 'Receive the holy Spirit ...'"
Jn. 20:21

Some translations say, "He breathed the Holy Spirit *into* them," so let's meditate upon that translation.

Take a few moments to *read* the text above again and internalize it, visually composing the scene. Imagine Christ in his resurrected radiance, divinely glowing. He faces you, slightly breathing forth his Spirit, which pulsates toward you visibly, instantly transforming you as you consciously breathe in his Spirit.

Reflect on Christ's resplendence, his serenity, his gift to you in the Holy Spirit and also how this Breath transforms you.

Respond by thanking him for his divine gifts and make a concrete and concerted response to him, in your meditation and also in your daily life.

Here are three ways we can apply this prayer by combining breathing and mind together.

1. Jesus = *Je-sus*: This is the Holy Name of the Savior, and when prayed syllable by syllable, slowly aligned with the breath, it can be both salvific and mentally calming! Je-sus ... breathing in and out slowly.

Just breathing in, breathing out—that's one, whole, total breath, slowly. Next, repeat this thiurty-two more times, calmly, perhaps using your hands or fingers to count and track so to alleviate your mind. (This hearkens the thirty-three breaths of the title!)

2. Breathing him/freeing within: Slowly count this saying on your fingers "counting" each syllable or saying, aligned with your entire in-and-out-breathing.

3. Simple counting: Each in and out breath, totally, count as "1," "2," "3" and so forth, one number-count for each entire breath. While this may seem contrived or bland at first, it frees and calms the mind in a very simple, casual, and natural way. We all know and count numbers in various situations and thus we all need simple methods to meditate. This is not complicated and is, after a time, helpful!

The point of all these practices is to calm the mind, still the soul, and gain rest and repose.

WATER

This meditation deals with Jesus meeting the Samaritan woman at the well, their dialogue, and Christ's subsequent manifestation as Godly life-giving water. Read John's Gospel, chapter 4:7-15 (Note, Jews do not associate with Samaritans, so for Jesus to ask her for a drink was very unusual.)

> *A woman of Samaria came to draw water. Jesus said to her, "Give me a drink." His disciples had gone into the town to buy food. The Samaritan woman said to him, "How can you, a Jew, ask me, a Samaritan woman, for a drink?" (For Jews use nothing in common with Samaritans.) Jesus answered and said to her, "If you knew the gift of God and who is saying to you, 'Give me a drink,' you would have asked him and he would have given you living water." [The woman] said to him, "Sir, you do not even have a bucket and the well is deep; where*

then can you get this living water? Are you greater than our father Jacob, who gave us this well and drank from it himself with his children and his flocks?" Jesus answered and said to her, "Everyone who drinks this water will be thirsty again; but whoever drinks the water I shall give will never thirst; the water I shall give will become in him a spring of water welling up to eternal life." The woman said to him, "Sir, give me this water, so that I may not be thirsty or have to keep coming here to draw water."

VISUALIZE Christ with a lady at a well in the countryside. Image a deep well with cool water below them, and then visualize, perhaps, fresh water coming straight from Jesus' side (not the well)—into you.

REFLECT on Christ at the well becoming the *"living* well"—himself as a vibrant source of everlasting water—cool, crystalline refreshing, pure. Think, oppositely, of the banality of endless repetition, going back again to a finite, incomplete, unfulfilling person, or, likewise a water well, or places or things that never totally fulfill us. And, contrastingly, meditate upon the infinity of Christ-life in you.

RESPOND by thanking him for this gift of quenching your spiritual thirsts and desires. Recall a time when you were thirsty and it was later quenched, and thank him, God, for this is what Jesus does to and for you in your meditative soul!

FOOD

One way or another, everybody's into food these days. Besides the basic need to just eat and survive, there seem to be a million cooking shows and celebrity chefs garnering attention and fame, not to mention, on the other hand, so many people trying to lose weight, dieting and exercising.

The following meditation is based on John 6, the famous account of the multiplication of the loaves and fishes and Jesus' speaking on another, higher level (a characteristic theme of St. John) about food and heaven and real, fulfilling desire. Jesus clearly describes himself as feeding people, us, through his life-giving body, himself, the Eucharist.

> *"I am the bread of life. Your ancestors ate the manna in the desert, but they died; this is the bread that comes down from heaven so that one may eat it and not die. I am the living bread that came down from heaven; whoever eats this bread will live forever; and the bread that I will give is my flesh for the life of the world."*
>
> *The Jews quarreled among themselves, saying, "How can this man give us [his] flesh to eat?" Jesus said to them, "Amen, amen, I say to you, unless you eat the flesh of the Son of Man and drink his blood, you do not have life within you. Whoever eats my flesh and drinks my blood has eternal life, and I will raise him on the last day. For my flesh is true food, and my blood is true drink. Whoever eats my flesh and drinks my blood remains in me and I in him. Just as the living Father sent me and I have life because of the Father, so also the one who feeds on me will have life because of me. This is the bread that came down from heaven. Unlike your ancestors who ate and still died, whoever eats this bread will live forever" (Jn. 6: 48–57).*

READ the passage in *lectio divina* fashion, not breezing through, but slowly, perhaps a couple times, allowing the spiritual words and meanings to embed within your soul by your receptive temperate relaxation. You may imagine Jesus as a kind of divine-human "bestowing-cascade" flowing and gracing of heavenly bread (himself) to you.

REFLECT on how life-giving Jesus is. He actually gives us his very self, and this flesh is our bread and life, supernatural sustenance to become one with us.

RESPOND by thanking him for his food, for his sacrificial and nourishing gift to you where both your body and soul are revived.

GOD AS TRINITY

The Catechism of the Catholic Church states: "The Trinity is the highest most central mystery of the Faith" (CCC 234). We should always remember in our meditation life, that our ultimate goal is God himself, always coming back to him amidst all the busyness, important pressing issues of the day. After all, what or who is more important than God himself?

The opening collect-prayer of the Trinity Sunday Mass proclaims:

> *"We acknowledge You as Trinity,*
> *We adore Your Unity,*
> *And the power of Your Majesty."*

Let's unpack and thus meditate upon that dense, classic, inspirational collect-prayer. Notice such liturgical prayers are both instructive and inspirational; they describe a mystery while also, hopefully, encouraging us to enter into it with abandon and love even while we do not fully comprehend it rationally.

Here are the essential elements of this prayer:

- Acknowledge
- Adore
- Unity
- Power/Majesty

This prayer is basically inspiring us to use both head and heart to synergize into God's realm of Divine Majesty.

As Christians, we are called to blend intellectual headiness, as in the "acknowledge" in the prayer to know God-as-Trinity, along with the heart-emotion-feelings to "adore" his Oneness-Unity so as to fully appreciate the majesty of God's power. We can summarize from this collect-prayer and Christian meditation itself a good, lifelong lesson: Emotion + Intellection = Holy Wholeness.

In your prayer and meditation (and all of life, really) synthesize your head and heart. Integrate thoughts and emotions into a spiritual unity so as to Love God-as-He-Is. Use and balance head and heart.

Now let's step it up a bit our Trinitarian meditation. *Perichoresis*, from the Greek, means, literally, "going around." This is one of the primary words in theology to describe God the Blessed Trinity, the Ultimate Mystery of life, and, specifically, to point to the inner relations of God himself.

God-as-Trinity is sometimes depicted in art and classic iconography, especially in Celtic-Irish culture, as an "organic-triangle" (alive and flowing, pulsating, versus an inert one). In other artwork, the Trinity is depicted as three angels supping together at a table. The point is that God is alive/flowing/eternally intertwining and also magnetizing, as he calls us into this, his Divine Life. All of these images show and symbolize oneness and life.

Now go back to one of these images above that can speak to you. We should be attracted to the image, one or another, and want to get involved in this spiritual phenomenon of God's Trinitarian life, both the divine persons themselves and His interconnectedness which are enticing.

ABC's of the Trinity

Here are three words that came to me that may help during your meditation:
- Attracting
- Blending
- Co-ascending

ATTRACTING means the Trinity calls, impels, and magnetizes us. God the Trinity is described both by a noun (God-as-Person) and as a verb, perichoresis—active, attracting, interacting. Like a dance, there is an affirmative outreach to us by God.

BLENDING suggests we become one with God the Trinity instead of worshiping him at a distance. Instead, we participate in God's nature by his mercy and divine friendship by his making us his adopted sons/daughters. CO-ASCENDING means we rise with him, God himself. As in mystical theologians' surmising, there is a spiral motion to the soul, a kind of metaphysical whirring of the spirit up into God himself. (For instance, medieval theologian St. Thomas Aquinas comments on the works of the ancient mystic Dionysius the Areopagite, emphasizing the soul's energy-life-attraction to things higher.) We are made for heaven and spiritual heights and so, as earthlings we don't (or shouldn't) just keep going round and round, horizontally, labyrinth-like, endlessly in the horizontal world. But, rather we should transcend, move upward by God's grace and become spiritually elevated. Our spirit-souls are carried up by his divine perichoresis and grace integrated into Divine Life!

The day before I first used this formulation and meditation, I was in the kitchen using a blender (yeah, dangerous I know!) to make a fruit drink. Yes, true story! This whirring machine of gyrating energy affected my subsequent meditation (doesn't life do that to you, too?). I reflected that the various elements of my smoothie drink—orange and apple, mango, beets and prunes and yogurt, coconut, ginger and strawberries—comprised a single drink. Watching ingredients whirring around in the blender reminded me of the old maxim on the American dollar: "From the many, One" ("E Pluribus Unum"). I watched all the elements eventually turning into one color (a beautiful burgundy red) and then spiral up to the top from an initial murky bottom thickness. Through the whirring and integration and elevation the fruits—and, likewise the individual soul in God's trinitarian life—become one and whole. This is how I image the perichoresis-union of God and our souls—blending/co-ascending, from the murky earth to heavenliness.

Remember that the Three Divine Persons are one uncreated essence and that these Persons, Father, Son and Holy Spirit, are neither inert nor autonomous but, rather, are mutually indwelling in one another.

Further, and uniquely for our purposes, these Divine Persons call us into their Life and Divine Love! We'll show you proof of this shortly, from God himself. But, for now, why do so few ever choose to believe him or, just as bad, fail to share this Good News and Divine-Trinitarian life relationship with others? This is our destiny; therefore, can you think of a better meditation to practice?

We are called as disciples, even here on Earth as crazy as it seems, to go *within* the Trinity, into Its inner divine dynamic life. So our meditation is focused on God himself and his dynamic love. If we "want to get there" we must first visualize him as he is and thereby imprint his Life and calling into our soul, mind, blood, and spiritual muscle cells. This world has a lot of alluring and ungodly pulls that can sidetrack us, so let's rather ascend to the highest union possible.

Part of perichoresis is "movement around"—as in the Divine persons intertwining and also penetrating within one another. And this inter-relatedness some speculate is for one Divine Person to allow or make room for the other Persons to enter into Its inner nature amid the infinite dynamism of the Trinitarian love. God-the-trinity is making room for us, also. Each Divine Person is inviting us into his Divine Life.

ALL THIS "THEOLOGY STUFF"

So, where does all this "theology stuff" lead us, or is it all mere speculation?

In John's Gospel, Jesus prays to his Heavenly Father for the disciples and all of us, uttering this marvelous mystifying news and promise:

> *"…so that they may all be one, as you, Father, are in me and I in you, that they also may be in us, that the world may believe that you sent me. And I have given them the glory you gave me, so that they may be one, as we are one" (John 17:21–22).*

Have you ever read more beautiful or promising words?

Jesus promises us not only union with God but "participation in the divine nature" (2 Pt. 1:4). And also, he proposes that that the glory that is inherent to God may be infused into us. Imagine, He-the-infinite, wise, uncreated Lord, wants to share with us little human beings who sin, his eternal glory, and life!

Now, since we should believe Jesus himself in the passage above, let us now "do" our meditation by *lectio* fashion.

READ the passage again, a couple times and/or visualize what Jesus is saying. You may imagine three dynamic rings together or a "vibrant triangle" or the whirring mixer, or three objects, three flowers, say, for example, merging together. Threeness coalescing into oneness is the dynamic key here for our meditation.

REFLECT on this by going into more detail on what you see, feel, and perceive, using your head, thinking about the sensual, visualized images. While you spiritually ponder and concentrate on the content, "don't get too heady" (rationalistic), but rather get affectively involved in the dynamic and kinetic relations of Divine Persons and communicating the Divine Life/glory to you.

RESPOND by talking back to God, thanking and praising him for all this glorious Divine life. This affection should, of course, be filled more with heartfulness and sentiments than heady thoughts and passive ideas at some level, with whatever image you use, say a letter within an envelope or a plant surging upward into a receptive, sunlit sky, we want to visualize and feel union, envelopment and individual surrender to the great whole or other parts. Our soul is flying to, and being received, into the Godhead!

"CHRISTIAN KOANS"

The parables of Jesus are excellent spiritual tools to train our intellects and hearts to meditate. Jesus' parables are narrative-stories that titillate the

KOANS

OVERFLOWING CUP OF TEA
The Zen Master poured his visitor's teacup full,
and then kept pouring.
The visitor watched until he could no longer restrain himself.
"It is overfull. No more will go in!"
"Like this cup," the Zen Master said,
"you are full of your own opinions and assumptions.
How can you learn truth until you first empty your cup?"

THE MOON CANNOT BE STOLEN
A thief entered the little hut of a Zen Master,
but discovered there was nothing to steal.
The Zen Master discovered the thief.
"You have come a long way to visit me," he told the prowler,
"and you should not return empty-handed.
Please take my clothes as a gift."
The thief was bewildered
but he took the clothes and slunk away.
The Zen Master sat naked, watching the moon.
"Poor fellow," he mused,
"I wish I could have given him this beautiful moon."
(From dancelight.com)

Koans are the uniquely Eastern, often Buddhist, presentation of a paradoxical problem (or case-story), and the solving thereof by a disciple tutored in them by a master. This was done in the East, Zen monasteries, and Taoist tribunes, through the inducement of a stilled mind into deeper meditation and then eventual transcending of the thinking, until arriving at the ultimate revelation of the unveiled answer by enlightenment liberation. This breakthrough

continue page 93 »

may come by way of slower (or gradual) means, or by a sudden enlightenment. The point is that reason is used and then broken through (if not broken down and then transcended) as a deeper revelation-manifestation is allowed or achieved.

These meditational accents are also found in Christianity in the process of the parables of Jesus in the Gospels and especially in Catholicism, with its strong emphasis on meditation and *lectio divina*, as well as graded steps of meditation leading to contemplation. More and more non-Catholic Christians and Catholics today emphasize "slow reading" of a (biblical) text, then pondering, and deeply meditating upon it. It is what we should all do in reading the holy Bible anyway, isn't it?

intellect and stimulate the heart and call these soul-faculties to a higher reality out of their previously sterile/stifling ways. The parables are like spiritual riddles/gateways into liberated ways of thinking and feeling.

As they usually do not have a "black or white" answer, they allow for subtle interpretation and imagination, creativity. They involve a versatile reading and application rather than a straightjacket solution, which is not really applicable to life's murkiness and slipperiness—and Jesus' intentions.

We could diagram Jesus' parable usage (and Eastern koans) in this way: Reason + Effort + Grace = Breakthrough / New Reality.

Jesus taught in parables so people would think through problems in a new way and shared truths he wanted them to treasure. That's the point: the effort was made intentionally so as to intellectually and spiritually arrive at a new solution, "out-of-the-box" thinking. He did not give static truth on a silver platter and deliver it in fortune-cookie-ready fashion to be quickly consumed and then forgotten. We need to use our human reason, our minds and hearts intensely in this pursuit, and grit our "intellectual teeth" in meditation, going deeper and focusing more. Also, we must strive to wait on the Lord and his mysterious ways for "answers" to various questions we have have.

We may gradually "open up" to various answers we encounter in the Gospel stories, works of theology, or parables. They do not always come according to our own timing or schedules, but we should intensely pursue the revelations deeply within. The word parable comes from the Greek, meaning "words around," so they are words near or proximate to a truth, not direct truth itself always or totally, but a story or words "about" a truth. The Lord is giving you these "words around," or nearby truth he wants you to pierce through, so that in stretching your mind, praying, and considering and meditating upon all this you become a new being—stretched in mind and heart Thus, you also develop a discipline of rightful holy meditative thinking that is different from mere rational, mere everyday thinking.

"Christian Koans," as we may call them, abound in our sacred tradition and they can be subjects of our meditation, deeper thinking and, hopefully, liberation from static ways of thinking. These are biblical paradoxes to berate (tantalize) and then liberate (free) us into new ways of being. The famous Catholic Christian G.K. Chesterton described them as such: "Truth standing on her head to attract attention."

By simply looking into the Christmas-time genre or Scripture we can think of many paradoxes to meditate upon:

- Begotten/not made: Jesus is eternally begotten of the Father, yet not created or fashioned. How can a being be "not made" yet be "begotten"? Think about that!

- Virgin/Mother: Blessed Mary is both a virgin and also a mother giving birth. … How is a lady both virginal and motherly in the same body?!

- Rich/Poor: Jesus is obviously divine-rich, but also poor in his way of birth and living, especially his birth in the cave of Bethlehem.

- God-Man: Christ is True God and truly human. He the

Christ is fully God and human—Easterners call him theandric. Meditate upon this divine-human "coalescence" and how we are invited to participate in both God's humanity and Godliness.

Now consider these other biblical paradoxes:

- "The message of the cross is foolishness to those who are perishing, but to us who are being saved it is the power of God" (1 Cor. 1:18). (Mediate upon true wisdom)

- "For everyone who exalts himself will be humbled, but the one who humbles himself will be exalted" (Lk. 14:11). (Humility versus haughtiness)

- "Whoever finds his life will lose it, and whoever loses his life for my sake will find it" (Mt. 10:39). (Lose and find)

- "Listen, my beloved brothers. Did not God choose those who are poor in the world to be rich in faith and heirs of the kingdom that he promised to those who love him?" (Jas. 2:5). (God's favor)

- "...for when I am weak, then I am strong" (2 Cor. 12:10). (Vulnerableness)

- "...always carrying about in the body the dying of Jesus, that the life of Jesus also may be manifested in our body" (2 Cor. 4:10). (Jesus within us)

- "It is more blessed to give than to receive" (Acts 20:35). (Freedom in giving vs. getting—greediness)

- "The last shall be first, and the first last" (Mt. 20:16). (Think: being first is attractive and rewarding, but be last in acknowledgment)

Sometimes, we need to twist up our minds, then untwist them. That's why we like riddles, fortune cookies, and paradoxes. By mental stress, intense focusing, and intellectual effort (sounds like meditation, doesn't it?), we can grow spiritually and, as we learn to "think outside the box" eventually we can break the box or eliminate it as we find or receive the "answer" to parables and mysteries. However, we have to work at it, with patience, mulling it over in our minds and in meditations, just as we have prescribed for you, doing the Three R's, of review, reflect, and respond.

READ or review. This means to pick up the Bible and read about Jesus or the above parables and other stories. (When you think about it, the whole Bible itself is a parable-paradox—God in search of man. Isn't that kind of backward—that man is supposed to be searching for God?) We must seek out those parable-stories like one uses toothpaste—ready to remedy-cleanse/purify us through a bustling/bristling effect. In this case, we want our brains to be bristled-purified. They may be sort of "locked-down" in states of no-growth and "same old" neuro-pathways of repetition. Do you always want instant answers that are spoon-fed to you, thus remaining in a kind of religious kindergarten of finger paints and fairy tales? Or, do you wish to venture into new neuropathways of spiritual truth that will liberate you after you sweat a little bit?

REFLECT on the spiritual issues of a parable, enigma, or mystery. This is an essential part of meditation since the root of this word *medita* means "to chew." In meditation we "spiritually munch" on an image or Bible story, spiritually struggle, become open to alternative solutions and pursue any and all thoughtful engagements with the story-parable. Relentlessly use your head and brainpower, searching and venturing into the Mind of God—Jesus. Remember: He gave these parables to his followers primarily to "grow them" and expand their understanding and receptivity of the Kingdom of Heaven, God himself (much wider and different than anyone could think), and discipleship and its costs (much more demanding and costlier than conceived). Therefore, we too need be willing to expand and adapt our minds, which is what meditative prayer does for us, as well!

RESPOND means to express sentiments to God, or about the parables/ spiritual problems, in order to both get into and out of an intellectual-spiritual chokehold because if God didn't give you these conundrums, you would still be in religious infancy and immaturity. And, if you can express to God, in the responding stage that you don't entirely understand the reviewed parable or spiritual problem—then join the club! The elusiveness and opacity of parables and prayerful problems will fuel your mind for the future, prevent intellectual pride, and help you worship God, who is, after all, above our understanding and beyond control. In prayer and meditation, we don't want to stay in a box or closed circuit circle whereby we presumably understand everything and draw down to our small, finite, unexpansive, fabricated God who we want to tame according to our petite and petty understanding.

Weird, cunning, elusive, offensive, tantalizing, and surpassing are some of the descriptors for these parables, along with our intense thinking upon them. Refashioning and re-configuring mind patterns denote the process of meditative prayer and parables when we contemplate them from our Lord Jesus Christ. One scholar says we are sure Jesus said these things because they are so unique, new and against religious custom that the Gospel writers or no one else could have invented them!

Many of these statements do not make much sense, humanly speaking. But they're God's ways, not ours, of getting our attention, expanding our thinking, and liberating our sterile lives! Obviously, there are many other beguiling forms like these, so dig into the Bible—and life—to stretch your brain and meditatively grow in wisdom.

THE MASS

The Catholic Mass (and other forms of Protestant worship, especially

Quaker and Anglican quietism), as celebrated through the centuries, has many different dispositions that help the spiritual seeker find and embrace God as well as cultivate an interior life. Through ritual (a liturgical action practiced over time, with heartfelt dispositions to help us worship God both within ourselves and in the liturgical service), these habits foster within the soul. There are many opportunities to practice both stillness and silence in the Mass and worship services, some of which include the following: kneeling, genuflecting, making the Sign of the Cross, walking and standing nobly, listening attentively, sitting upright, etc. (Remember: "don't slouch at Mass," as mom used to command!). These are all physical postures that affect our metaphysical selves and spiriting insides and express worship and community life.

BIBLE READINGS

When we hear the Old Testament and/or Gospel reading at Mass or a worship service, we may get distracted; we could be thinking about the afternoon soccer match or current hunger pains. We're in the midst of the most sublime service and it seess sometimes were "going pedestrian." Happens all the time—to everyone. So...

Here is one of the best pearls of wisdom ever I've heard about the Mass, from a pastor-priest friend: simply, saliently and slowly within, repeat the words of the reading done by the lector or prayers prayed by the priest or minister under your breath. Stay attentive to what is being proclaimed so you may hear deeply and then internalize the spoken words—whether prayers, the Bible or sermon, or song, and embed intimately within head and heart. In a way, this is part of *lectio divina* and liturgical meditation. Do this and you will stay on spiritual target. Repeat the words of the Mass within!

There are also brief pauses during the Mass that offer time for prayer: reflection after the homily (sermon), while looking at the Lamb of God in the Sacred Host held aloft just after consecration, and following holy Communion, etc. These are pauses where the attendee can briefly meditate and deepen the actions celebrated in the Mass instead of "just going through the motions."

During Communion time at our church, I am always inspired and still slightly amazed at the eloquent, deep silence, and stillness of a hundred-plus people attending. You can hear the proverbial pious pin drop. This is not accidental: it doesn't just happen but rather comes about by Mass attendees consciously and conscientiously through healthy living, a life of silence and stillness, communal prayer, mental and shared witness and practice, and of course, love of God. How many times a week does a person get to be still with a hundred other people? Rarely? Never? We need to preserve this stillness and silence in our church, as basically no other institutions are teaching or preserving this sacred discipline

For some Catholics today, this practice and disposition of stillness and silence (especially in an increasingly activist world and church with loss of such disciplines) may seem "newish" for many following Vatican Council II (1962-1965), which, of course, changed the language of the Mass from the normative Latin, and with the priest facing the congregation and, so forth. The first text of the Council was "Sacrosanctum Concilium" which has sometimes been misperceived and mistaught, thus de-linking the rich tradition of the past, emphasizing mystery and meditation, for instance, and the Mass today. Much of the background of the text and emphasis upon active participation in specific have a historical background rooted precisely in internal recollection first and then this interiority expressed through outer-active forms. If one does not have the internal discipline that we have been stressing all along, then outer expressions are vain and hollow. Therefore, we need both practices in our approach to the Mass and worship, not an either/or approach—either extremes of hoopla or monasticism. We must seek the "radical middle" of both/and—both internal quietude and external action—as does Catholicism in its many forms.

LIFE OF MEDITATION

Another pearl of wisdom I've learned from monastic life summarizes eloquently and beautifully what meditation is:

Abbot Bernard spoke to the monks about Isaiah's vision (of the Lord in glory). ... But for this present, he said there is another vision of that same Lord that should be the focus of our contemplation: the image of the suffering Servant, the Leper, the One struck by God. This was a dangerous sort of contemplation, for it meant more, much more than an objective viewing of that leper from a comfortable distance. For Bernard, as for the monks he taught, to contemplate meant to intend to be transformed into the likeness of the object contemplated. To gaze fixedly upon Jesus in the lowly economy of salvation meant to become oneself what Jesus is.

William of St. Thierry, a Trappist monk, enunciated a descriptive formula that eloquently describes our life of meditation: "ut igatur in nobis quod legitur in nobis." "That what we read about may be realized within us." (Chrysogonus Waddell in Cistercian Studies vol 23: 1988-1)

MEDITATION-VISUALIZATION

"Then there appeared to them tongues as of fire,
which parted and came to rest on each one of them.
And they were all filled with the Holy Spirit"
(Acts 2:3-4).

The meditation I offer for you here is:
- Dove descending
- Aura cleansing

Visualize the Holy Spirit as a light-colored dove or vibrant spiritual wind coming from heaven, to you, perhaps to the top of your head. Now, visualize the Dove-Spirit-Wind entering into you, penetrating, and flowing down within your whole body. God-the-Spirit is divinizing your entire body-being. This divine interaction cleanses you, all your soul and body.

Let us recall that the word *aura* is from the Greek and Latin, meaning wind, breeze, air, and may symbolize in each of us, individual persons, in a spiritual way, a surrounding, emanating spirit that exudes from each person. (We have phrases to express this, such as "There's an air about him" or "I got good vibes from her," etc.) This "spirit" of ours can obviously become contaminated. So, we need the penetrating breath of God, the Spirit-Dove to cleanse us, our spirits. Just as we have sometimes been infiltrated with evil in our spirits, we can also be cleansed and divinized with the purifying Holy Spirit.

So, practice, pray.

Breathe in and out slowly, become relaxed, restore.

- Dove descending—imagine him, the Holy Spirit, coming in you, descending and instantly healing you

- Aura-cleansing—your whole being cleansed, restored re-created

As we know, there is lots of debris—"mental clots" and "spiritual residues" and all kinds of junk that suffocate and darken our bodies and beings. We all need godly purification. Therefore, you may envision within yourself a kind of "inner swamp" darkened by tar and mud and dirty water—all results of your sins and attachments, emotional-spiritual idolizing, the accrued content of past actions and reactions. We need this "Dove descending-Holy Spirit" to cleanse all this and we cannot do it without God's spiritual Light and Love within us. We need to be liberated by God, spiritually showered from all the bad of the world and what we have done ourselves, so that we may accumulate the Divine Spirit-Breath Light for refreshment.

Let your inner soul transform into that of God's image, showered and cleaned, totally cleansed, radiant!

ACTIVE PRAYER AND MINDFULNESS

During your day, as you grow in strength of concentration and love of God, and gaining inner silence and simplicity, you may want to pray and practice this aspiration: *Age quod aegis*. It's simple and elegant in its Latin proposition. It means "do what you are doing." Translation: don't multitask and split or stress your mind. While doing the dishes—do the dishes. While talking to your spouse—talk to your spouse.

I was on a hike one time, all by myself in the beautiful western Maryland mountains. I became distracted (what else is new?), thinking of appointments and the proverbial shopping list of things I had to do, various worries and so forth. I gradually became aware of the fact that I was obviously missing out on all the surroundings God made and provided so perfectly for me. I was "being robbed"! So, I eventually formulated the basic idea/phrases below, which have stuck with me for decades throughout various similar situations.

- Nothing lacking
- Nothing distracting
- All things divinely interacting

Let's explore that, one line at a time:

NOTHING LACKING: This means, essentially, there's nothing I need when I'm grounded in this particular, present moment, whether the moment is occurring in nature, or in church or with friends. There's nothing in those situations that I need so I could say, "I already have everything I need, now." In other words, I'm not daydreaming about something or someone else.

NOTHING DISTRACTING: There's nothing around me or, just as importantly, nothing within my head, that is "robbing" me of, or subtracting from, the present moment. I'm focused on the here and now, nothing else.

ALL THINGS DIVINELY INTERACTING: Now, cleared for "at-one-moment," I can sensually see, touch, taste, and feel all the elements of this unique, unrepeatable event of now-ness, as divinely-providentially orchestrated, and blended together perfectly for me and my enjoyment.

God has perfectly blended all elements nearby us while on a hike or in the backyard; it's our Christian job to be present to and enjoy his creation!

Like all aspirations and mantras, this one above is a "spiritual bridge," and to be used, crossed and then "ditched"! This particular aspiration enables/links/bridges us into the present moment—away from anxieties and other preoccupations—and then, thus focused, we embrace and immerse ourselves in the content actuality of the moment.

As you enter a situation—at work, on a neighborhood playground, in school or in a beautiful field—you may use this aspiration until you are relaxed, fully present and thus, more deeply engaged in the situation. Eventually, faithfully saying the aspiration may—and this where it becomes ironic—even block you from truly being there precisely because you are saying, actively intending the aspiration, thus kind of blocking you from real, deeper immersion into the uniqueness of the situation. You're on the "bridge," not over it! The bridge is intended to help you cross over to another deeper reality, in this case, the present moment—that's what bridges do, transport you not to stay stuck. Got it?

As in many aspects of living, a balance is needed—in this case between using the aspiration and "crossing over into its intended present-moment reality." Use the saying until you don't need to use it, wherein, in this instance, the divine interacting things are "speaking" to you "louder" than the aspiration and you have successfully immersed yourself in the present moment's reality!

OASIS WITHIN

We read about Ezekiel, the prophet in his book of the Old Testament, and of God reviving Israel and, in some way, all of us today.

The hand of the Lord came upon me, and he led me out in the spirit of the Lord and set me in the center of the broad valley. It was filled with bones. He made me walk among them in every direction. So many lay on the surface of the valley! How dry they were! He asked me: "Son of man, can these bones come back to life?" "Lord God," I answered, "you alone know that." Then he said to me: "Prophesy over these bones, and say to them: Dry bones, hear the word of the Lord!"... I prophesied as he commanded me, and the breath entered them; they came to life and stood on their feet, a vast army. He said to me: "Son of man, these bones are the whole house of Israel! They are saying, 'Our bones are dried up, our hope is lost, and we are cut off.' Therefore, prophesy and say to them: 'Thus says the Lord God: Look! I am going to open your graves; I will make you come up out of your graves, my people, and bring you back to the land of Israel. You shall know that I am the Lord, when I open your graves and make you come up out of them, my people! I will put my spirit in you that you may come to life, and I will settle you in your land. Then you shall know that I am the Lord. I have spoken; I will do it—oracle of the Lord'" (Ez. 37: 1-4, 10-14).

This is one of my favorite stories in the Bible. I think one can't not like it, as it symbolizes us in that we sometimes grow dry in life and need to be revived by God himself. The story further shows how He is ever-faithful to his creations, even though we are like "dry bones"—sinful or fatigued sludge traipsing through life.

We should desire to breathe in God and become new creations. As we also have seen and prayed before, Jesus himself breathed the Holy

Spirit upon the apostles, saying, "Receive the Holy Spirit..." (Jn 20:21ff). So, first, before this, there was this Divine Breath emitted in Creation, God breathing into Adam, or slime(!); then upon the prophet Ezekiel; and then by Jesus himself to the apostles (who sent the Spirit to all of us), then the church and sacraments and priests.

The ego wants to flee God, meditation, and focus. We want to make meditation and prayer "ego-friendly, comfortable," or just stay busy and preoccupied and in control. Now picture an oasis, or a verdant green garden to which you are instantly attracted. One you can visualize easily within. Imagine this lush paradise within. Now think and feel that your soul, body, and mind need Christ who is the lushness of this Garden of Eden. We mortals are lost and are always trying to regain this "Garden-Oasis"—and He is Celestial Life and liveliness of such Garden—interiorly, within us.

Breathing Him/Oasis within
BREATHE slowly and visualize, through long, stretching, relaxed breaths, both Christ the God-Man and an oasis as he is entering you, pervading you, greening you within. This "oasis" pulsates within and nourishes, sustains and heals you.

IMAGE the radiant Christ within you, amidst this primal-precious Garden. Breathe thirty-three breaths of him—his being intimately within, in deeper, longer, rhythmic breaths.

The important thing is to INTERNALIZE the Garden and God living within you. "It becomes you" because God is overflowing and you are now one with it, him, the Garden and its greeing, healing effects.

RECALL that Christ died on a tree and trees grow in gardens and forests, and thus this redemptive Tree of Life reverses the Tree of sin.

Breathe slowly, allowing the Garden and God to fertilize you within.

LOVE

St. Paul of the Cross, German spiritual writer and missionary, writes: "Love turns the lover into the Beloved." As we have previously stated, attested by St. Peter's letter (2 Pt. 1:4), we are called to become like God, even partake of His divine nature, and this is the process called *theosis* or divinization, and this mystic sentiment is much heralded in Catholic-Christian mystical theology. Why? Because, it is from the Bible and our ancient heritage. St. John the Apostle, himself, states: "Beloved, we are God's children now; what we shall be has not yet been revealed. We do know that when it is revealed we shall be like him, for we shall see him as he is. Everyone who has this hope based on him makes himself pure, as he is pure" (1 Jn. 3:2-3).

In St. John's "realized eschatology," God's Kingdom and presence is not just in the future or after death, but in the present-now; so while we are living our normal lives before Heaven, this "glory" of Christ's can manifest in his disciples, ourselves, now. Why wait? God promises us glory now. And, as Christians, while we must be humble and rely on grace (you've learned that lesson, from this *Little Book* by now, yes?), we are also called to God-likeness.

Let us now meditate upon this aspiration—Love:

Turn me into Thee.

LOVE: You, the disciple, are seeking God, Who himself is love (see: 1 Jn. 4:16), and who is both a personal being and "activity." Let's explain. Jesus Christ sums up both aspects of God—that He is a personal being *and* activity—when He says to his fellow Jews, "My Father is at work until now, so I am at work" (Jn. 5:17). Also, St. Paul uses this eloquent both/and paradox of theology when he proclaims, "God is a consuming fire" (Heb. 12: 29). In this meditation on "Love," we desire God-as-action, to interact with us. You may visualize God-Love as fire, breathing, or as the eloquent gaze of Jesus upon the rich young disciple before he gave him the rough news: "Jesus, looking at him, loved him and said to him, 'You are lacking in one thing. Go, sell what you have, and give to [the] poor and you will have treasure in heaven; then come, follow me'" (Mk. 10:21). Here, the point in all these is activity, Divine Love-as-motion, love is an action-verb-movement (though God is just as much a being-pronoun, proper name). With regard to this type of divine and elegant love, Dante eloquently stated in the ending of The Divine Comedy, "Love that moves the sun and the other stars" (Paradiso: XXXIII).

TURN: The emphasis here, in this word, is on motion/change/transformation. God is the agent of change and we are the subjects. Other words to meditate upon include infiltrate (He comes into us); elevate (He lifts us above this world); emancipate (God frees us from sin/self-love). You may imagine a drop of water falling into an ocean of warm, salt water. The drop turns into and becomes the ocean-water of salt. The drop becomes a new reality. Also, visualize the season of spring, previously sleeping in winter and by the sun's powers waking up and protruding from the running sap; thus, flowering-forth. Likewise, God changes us in a divine-human transformation.

ME: This word centers on "self," the one undergoing change, yourself. While we certainly have a high calling to God-likeness, herein we recall we are all sinners: "…all have sinned and are deprived of the glory of God (Rm. 3:23). You can visualize, as I did initially in doing this meditation, a large block of marble-stone, in which we are frozen. This is what sin does to us—freezes and imprisons us. So, seek God's help, as we are creatures in need of a saving-transforming Creator. We are released from the stone and become fully alive.

INTO: Enter into and embrace God to finalize-complete the process. We are called into God's life, into his nature, and into his ways.

THEE: This means God himself and here we may ponder and imagine God-as-Person, pronoun versus verb, God-as-Be-ing. He is a Trinity of Divine Persons and we can enter into, by his grace, that enveloping Love. Visualize a "Divine envelope," your soul entering Its pristineness. He, God, is all around, surrounding you. But let's admit and mean it: it's impossible to become like him or even get near him without his grace and help! God is both our goal and our transformative agent to help us achieve our goal. Just as Love is both noun and verb, God is both a being and pure-actuality-verb.

Slowly, repeat this saying within as you pray-meditate. Then, perhaps, let it drop-disappear after some time, thus imagining a drop into an ocean, or the flower emerging from a tree. Allow your soul to transform into God's grace and godliness.

LECTIO DIVINA

We've talked much about *lectio divina*, so here are a couple of healing meditations based on this meditation form.

HEALING WATER

"Indeed, the water I give him will become in him
a fount of water springing up to eternal life"
—*Jn. 4:14.*

"The Lamb upon the throne is the light"
—*Rev. 21:23.*

If there's one thing we need in life and that Jesus delivers, it is healing. Wherever he went, he healed. More than thirty passages in Scripture describe Jesus healing someone, whether physical or supernatural. It's natural to ask the question: Why did he heal so much—and exorcise demons from so many people? The simple answer is that we are sick; we are sometimes plagued by bad spirits; we are attached or even addicted to bad things, harmful people and morals and behaviors. And though we

THE ROSARY

This famous and beautiful devotion is both a dynamic and lingering meditation upon the twenty mysteries of Jesus' life, Passion, and after-life. It is the New Testament of the Bible, extended to us through devotional means, including scriptural meditation, imaging within, and sacred repetition. Thus, a devotee practices many spiritual facets at one time.

The "Hail Mary" actually comes from the Bible (Lk. 1:28), where the Virgin Mary is approached by the angel Gabriel, announcing to her that she will be the Mother of God. Thus, we have the term "Annunciation" and all the famous painting-depictions.

The word *rosary* comes from the Latin, meaning "garland of roses" as the rose is a cherished symbol of the Blessed Virgin. While St. Dominic is said to have received it from the Virgin Mary in the 13th century (the traditional date is 1214), various prayers surrounding it were already used and familiar to many Christians, but not in the exact form as we know the rosary today. Many speculate that a kind of rosary "rope" was established by some Desert Fathers in Egypt in the fourth century and passed on to the West. The idea back then, as today, was focusedness, physical help in and through a sacramental such as the rosary-rope and beads, and constant prayer.

Amidst varied historical accounts (known and contested) about the rosary, let us cut to the quick and establish a few important points:

- It is meant to increase devotion to Christ's Life and Mother Mary, in that order.

- It is also a prayer of the heart and head, as so we need to think about mysteries and love their meaning deeply and not just lightly.

- Many strive to pray it often and to make it a holy habit throughout their lives, so this virtuous practice can assist us, too!

continue page 110 »

- Within the rosary is a balance between repetition and deep prayer-reflection, which can be very difficult to learn at first but can be embraced with dedication.

- One thing we want to avoid, amidst all this, is rote repetition. We can either just say the words of the rosary, mindlessly, or sacredly say and mean them repetitively and intentionally with our heart. Pope St. John Paul II encouraged us to pray the rosary contemplatively, not race through it like an auctioneer.

Learn to pray the rosary for itself, but also for the spiritual disciplines it teaches you: repetition with depth, constant prayer, and love of God and Mary as well as learning the Bible.

Visualize within yourself the mystery, for instance, the birth of Jesus or his Crucifixion or his Transfiguration. Then, ask Mary to help you ponder that particular scene and holy event—to enter into it.

I advise you to "start small and build tall." You may begin by praying a decade a day and gradually increase to the total five decades in one session. The core of the rosary is, really, the decade, encompassed by the Our Father, ten Hail Mary's, and Glory Be. Strive to pray a decade contemplatively, adding more over time with great love and devotion.

are increasingly ignorant of this fact that ancients knew intimately, we become what we do. Acidic actions lead to disintegrating disciples. But we can be healed through meditation because meditation is an internal and concentrating exercise in allowing God to deeply change us.

It is very important to realize this sickness of sin and corruption is not only moral, external, but it is metaphysical, harming our insides, our soul. Thus, once again, through *lectio divina*, meditation, we can have our insides healed. Jesus knows this and so does the Catholic Church, as exemplified by the antidotes including the healing sacraments, including the eating of Christ's Flesh and drinking of His Blood in the Eucharist as a reversal of the sickness. As Jesus says in John 6:55, "My Flesh is real food and My Blood real drink." Notice that the medicine as indicated by the Bible and taught by the Catholic Church is a systemic, ongoing effort allowing and accessing Christ *within* us and not just added onto, our intellectual heads.

Now, briefly ponder this Jesus-story from the Bible and just who he was:

> *"The whole multitude sought to touch Him (Jesus):*
> *for there went virtue-power out of Him,*
> *and healed them all"*
> *(Luke 6: 19 KJV).*

This clearly demonstrates an instance of Jesus-the-metaphysical when he is *radiating* his powers for the sick. Are you absorbing them within?

Now, let's practice lectio divina, divine reading, and meditate with God's words, images, and healing stories. Read the passage of Ezekiel through very slowly. Reflect upon it by using your mind and thoughts. Respond by giving affections and emotions over to God and his way that you have pondered.

Visualize cleansing water

Then he brought me back to the door of the temple, and behold, water was issuing from below the threshold of the temple toward the east (for the temple faced east). The water was flowing down from below the south end of the threshold of the temple, south of the altar. Then he brought me out by way of the north gate and led me around on the outside to the outer gate that faces toward the east; and behold, the water was trickling out on the south side. Going on eastward with a measuring line in his hand, the man measured a thousand cubits, and then led me through the water, and it was ankle-deep. Again he measured a thousand, and led me through the water, and it was knee-deep. Again he measured a thousand, and led me through the water, and it was waist-deep. Again he measured a thousand, and it was a river that I could not pass through, for the water had risen. It was deep enough to swim in, a river that could not be passed through. (Ez. 47: 1-12 ESV).

Read the passage again, this time more slowly. Put yourself in the reading-text and become part of it. Reflect on how you yourself gently wade into that water, healing, godly water. Then respond, in your meditation, as water overflows upon and all around you and you are liberated from any shackles and sicknesses. Your soul is changed, gladsome, and elevated. That is healing water you enter *into.*

Thus, it's no mistake or coincidence that Jesus went into the River Jordan for baptism, and so invites you to cleansing in similar ways. Now visualize the liberating water within—as Jesus intimates in John 4—*flowing within.* This transition is classic: from outer to inner, external to internal; extraversion to introversion, God's life is within you.

We need cleansing *interiorly.* So, let's now ponder, via *lectio divina* and God's word:

Jesus answered, "If you knew the gift of God and who is asking you for a drink, you would have asked Him, and He would have given you living water." "Sir," the woman replied, "You have nothing to draw with and the well is deep. Where then will you get this living water?" ... Jesus said to her, "Everyone who drinks this water will be thirsty again. But whoever drinks the water I give him will never thirst. Indeed, the water I give him will become in him a fount of water springing up to eternal life." The woman said to Him, "Sir, give me this water so that I will not get thirsty and have to keep coming here to draw water." (Jn. 4:10-15)

Read the passage again, slowly. Reflect on how Jesus as divine water flows within you. And then respond. The refreshing, cleansing, and healing water is within you and so you may respond by embracing Him-the-Water in gratefulness, with heartfelt emotion and commitment to return to this center within, Christ the life-giving water!

THE DIVINE LAMB

Another image we can use in meditation is the Divine Lamb, symbolizing Jesus. The lamb is a typical and archetypal symbol that symbolizes the scapegoat-ransom for us sinners in exchange for the punishment of our sins. Once again, that Lamb, Jesus Christ, in our view and spiritual lives, is not only external but also internal, especially in the Catholic Mass, as we consume and embrace the Lamb within. As we pray in the Mass and as we view the priest holding aloft the consecrated eucharistic host, we say the following (and the following is a biblical response):

"Lord I am not worthy to have you come under my roof,
but only the word and my soul shall be healed" (Mt. 8:8).

These verses elucidate the Lord Jesus as living and loving:

"Behold the lamb of God who takes away the sins of the world"
(Jn. 1:29).

"Then I saw a Lamb who appeared to have been slain, standing
in the center of the throne, encircled by the four living creatures
and the elders" (Rev. 5:6).

"The throne of God and of the Lamb will be in the city, and his
servants will serve him. They will see his face, and his name
will be on their foreheads. There will be no more night. They
will not need the light of a lamp or the light of the sun, for the
Lord God will give them light. And they will reign for ever
and ever" (Rev. 22:3-5).

"The city does not need the sun or the moon to shine on it,
for the glory of God gives it light, and the Lamb is its lamp"
(Rev. 21:23).

Now, for our meditation, *lectio divina* style, dwell upon the previous Bible texts:

Glowing Lamb
healing-flowing
into my inner man

(You may substitute "inner land" in the last line instead of "inner man.")

The Lamb of God, Jesus Christ, in the Book of Revelation is light-filled, radiant, and undulating, giving us his divine grace. He is NOT a static symbol. He is pulsating and alive.

The Divine Light "pipelines" right into your heart, soul, your whole body.

"Inner" means your heart and soul, your blood and entire internal system of life, Christ the glowing-healing Lamb is in you!

Read the passages above or use the aspiration I have created. Reflect upon the passage or aspiration, and respond with heartfulness.

CHAPTER SIX

"THEOLOGY STUFF" TO REALITY

"AND LET THE BEAUTY OF THE LORD OUR
GOD BE ON US: AND ESTABLISH THOU
THE WORK OF OUR HANDS ON US; YES,
THE WORK OF OUR HANDS ESTABLISH THOU IT"
(PS. 90:17—AMERICAN KING JAMES BIBLE)

On the cover of this book is a photograph of Kenai Peninsula in Alaska, where I made a summer pilgrimage. We may recall in viewing this St. Thomas Aquinas's saying, "God is the artist and the universe is his work of art." God fashioned that beautiful frontier of Alaska and also is fashioning an artwork out of you, and especially through meditation, you are learning to be his handiwork!

We've been on the most serious and serene tour of life—of the mind and soul! Hopefully we've learned many ways to meditate, from the "Three R's" (remember: Read, Reflect, Respond) to the "Three T's" (Think, Then Thank, by using head and heart, thoughts and emotions), but, also that it is the Lord God, the Divine Trinity, whom we are to think about and thank the most, not get stuck on ourselves or our disciplines or, even, however necessary to acknowledge, our sinful shortcomings. The purpose of all this is not just our bliss, but him, the Glory of the Lord!

For full disclosure: I'm neither a Ph.D. nor a trained spiritual director. I'm just a simple parish priest (or at least trying to be). However, if you think about it (and I have), to learn or even teach spirituality, you don't really need to be some religious pinhead or trained monk or Catholic "shaman," approved by the Vatican to do such. After all, most of what we will learn is common sense, "basic Spirituality 101" and, besides, we have the Holy Spirit to guide us and some 2,000 years of super-sacred Catholic Christian Tradition to help us on our journey. In this book, I've tried to amalgamate everything together in simplicity so that you can practice it.

While writing this book, I myself struggled with meditation, stillness, and focus. I found it a challenge to actually just sit, be silent, and focus for my full hour in the morning and then at night. After decades of meditation, it seemed that I was slipping, recently—compromising my holy hour time and not focusing as I should.

There were days I could hardly focus, and yet other days filled with some equanimity. Other times, I would just have my coffee, thinking spiritual thoughts and pray in between sips of the mojo. Gradually, I kept on, persevered. Yet, I had somehow lost the fervor—and discipline—and became, basically, lazy—a spiritual slacker without concentration and inner directedness while distracted by the outer world. I was showing up for prayer and meditation, taking the time, but not inwardly focused enough or loving in a disciplined way. However, I kept faith in the Lord Jesus' promise and that the gift of interior prayer would not be taken from me (see: Lk. 10:40).

Thus, dear reader, this *Little Book* stresses concentration and love of the Lord and his ways of spirituality, and a discipline blended with heartfulness, focus, and attentiveness. That is what meditation is. It is not scattered religious refraction and nebulous reflection, nor mindless meddling (which is what I was tending toward and, therefore, found difficult to get back to that which was, seemingly, so natural before). We must all foster interior stillness and focus, no matter the challenges!

With that, I leave you with ten tips for the interior life:

1. Pray/Meditate: Take ten to twenty minutes each day, preferably at morning and/or night, to meditate, which means, as you now know, focused love upon the Lord God. Practice holy silence and stillness as best you can every day even before you get there. Be unrelenting. It's about God and your soul's growth!

2. Read the Bible: Learn to integrate the Bible, its counsels into your life. Remember, "Your word is a lamp unto my feet" (Ps. 119). *Lectio divina*—divine reading—is best lived by ingesting the Word into you. Practice daily.

3. Attend Mass or worship service with biblical readings and prayers: become an adorer often. *Sursum corda*—lift up your heart to the Lord in the elevation of liturgical prayer and meditation.

4. Sacramental: Put holy pictures/medals/icons around your house, workstation, and car. These remind you that you are a creature of God and need to commune and communicate with him by these reminders.

5. Spiritual Reading: Take/make ten minutes a day of a saint's writings, classical works, or the Catechism into your prayer and interior life.

6. Subtract: Get rid of junk, both outside and inside—in your house and in your head. Turn off TV, radio, and phone. Wean yourself from constant communication with the world and commune with the Creator of the world.

7. Retreat: Get away for a day or a week each year. During the rest of the year make some regular getaway, to a nearby park or out of way place, to sit, meditate, and rest awhile (See Mk. 6.31).

8. Practice the presence of God: In each moment, more deeply and mindfully consider and appreciate what you are seeing, doing, gently focusing on that sacred time and place you are in God's holy presence and releasing all other thoughts.

9. Use aspirations/mantras: repeat reverently your sacred word or phrase that links you to God and holy mindfulness.

10. Cultivate ESP: E is for an embrace, S is for stillness (of the body and chattering mind), and P is for persevering: Embrace stillness, perseveringly. The thing is, when it comes to prayer, conversation with God, we don't always have ESP as we are distracted. Prayer and meditation take ESP!

So, this, above in ten points, is my advice to you, friend. Show up each day, grab your Bible verse or sacred icon, lean into focusing on the Lord, and accept the challenges of meditation and deepened prayer. This is God's way of testing and strengthening your inner life. Keep on, persevere, never give up, and don't slack. You need discipline whose source is your head and fervor from your heart—and God's grace. Keep and cultivate this sacred balance.

In short—meditate. Love God and deepen your relationship with him.

"We meditate before, during and after everything we do. The prophet says: 'I will pray, and then I will understand.' This is the way we can easily overcome the countless difficulties we have to face day after day, which, after all, are part of our work. In meditation, we find the strength to bring Christ to birth in ourselves and in others" (St. Charles Borromeo).

FINAL THOUGHTS

W hen I was reviewing the manuscript of this *Little Book*, my loving mother died. I was somewhat prepared for this event but still experienced both tremendous sadness and joy at the passing of her life from this world to the eternal. She was 83 and I was blessed to have her so long, since she survived ten good years on oxygen, with COPD draining her body. When she finally passed after weeks of acute suffering, it was truly a blessing, very peaceful. I now share some blessings I learned, meditatively, through this difficult experience.

For two weeks before my mother died, she was struggling in the hospital. Through those days, thanks to my daily prayer regimen, I persevered in prayer. But it wasn't easy. So, here are three things I learned from this difficult time:

1. Focus: many times during my meditation hours I would get distracted, agitated—naturally, of course with Mom's condition and all the challenges with family and medical issues. I learned that I needed help in focusing, and that "help" came in the form of the icon Divine Mercy card, which was both in Mom's hospital room and at her home where I spent many days and nights. I invite you to search

for the icon of Divine Mercy online and you will see the resurrected Jesus with divine light emanating from His body, in an inviting open bodily manner, welcoming you, the viewer-worshipper. Having the icon in front of me, focused me and my flitting mind, calming me. Eventually, an old mantra-aspiration came to me, which I often prayed: *Christ's pulsating light / breathe in delight.* My suggestion to you is when you find it hard to pray, use an icon, crucifix or holy card or medal, something that is attractive to you, to concentrate your powerful but fallen and sometimes frenzied mind! The depicted Christ in the icon, with his streaming light, helped me through this challenging experience and such a sacramental-icon can help you. Visualization methods imprint new neural life in the mind and also, in the case of holy meditations, Divine Love!

2. *Jesus, I trust in You!* When I was with Dad at Mom's bedside, many, many times, we prayed this aspiration. We all knew the aspiration so it was a friendly and familiar "sacred touchstone" for us to pray. A few times I stayed overnight to help Mom and as she woke up in the night, we would pray that small, powerful prayer. You can pray it in your meditation time or walking down the street or whenever you have need.

3. The funeral Mass I said for my mother was beautiful and flawless. Though it was intense and somewhat sorrowful, it was also mystical and joyful. I somehow knew that despite my sadness I would be able to say the Mass because I had been a priest almost thirty years, and said other sad and difficult Masses through challenged and varied situations. I knew those prior, challenging experiences would help me with my mom's funeral. I also knew my disciplined prayer-meditation life helped and continues to help. Through the daily ritual I have developed in quiet, meditative prayer, the inner discipline and concentrative focus I have developed—(but still need to work on, for sure!)—I was able to pray through my mother's

Mass, and I even could sing certain parts of it. The daily, meditative discipline of so many years fueled me into my mother's liturgy and gave me confidence and concrete acts of prayerfulness to offer the best for her and God.

As they say, good can come out of difficulty (see: Rm. 8: 28), and even from this experience of darkness in my mother's passing. To you, dear meditator-friend, I encourage you to focus and maintain ongoing aspirational prayer—to love God more, and your neighbor also! All this gathered and accumulated discipline will help you in the unforeseen, challenging events of life that happen to all of us. Through each breath, may the Lord fashion you more and more into His Divine Nature (2 Pt. 1:4) and may you pray, as did St. Francis of Assisi, "Lord, make me an instrument of your peace"!

KEEP PRAYING!

ABOUT THE AUTHOR

Photo by Tom McCarthy Jr. | CR Media

Rev. John J. Lombardi, pictured above in western Maryland on a 100-mile walk for religious freedom, is pastor of St. Peter Church, Hancock, and St. Patrick Church, Little Orleans, Md. He was born in 1960 in Baltimore to Rose and William Lombardi, the fourth of five children. He had a happy childhood growing up in Timonium, Md., attending public schools with varied activities, including religion and Mass, various sports, neighborhood fun and lots of family gatherings of Italian and Polish heritage of his parents.

Later in life, he drifted away from God, the Catholic Church and found various troubles and un-spiritual things to get into, then attended Dulaney Senior High school and Towson State University, majoring in journalism and philosophy.

He eventually found his vocation to the priesthood through studies in college and help from laypersons and priests and many others. He then decided to attend The Catholic University of America in Washington, D.C., gaining a Master of Theology there, and was ordained a priest in 1988 in the Baltimore Archdiocese. He was assigned to St. Mary's Church in his hometown of Baltimore City, then went to India on a summer sabbatical and worked with Mother Teresa. He desires to return as he experienced many profound lessons and the "art of adventure," traveling the Indian subcontinent.

He also served in parishes in Perry Hall-Baltimore; Randallstown; St. Elizabeth Nursing Home, Baltimore; and at the National Shrine Grotto of Lourdes-Mount St. Mary's University in Emmitsburg, Md.

He now serves in Hancock, in western Maryland, where it is beautiful not only for prayer and contemplation but also for hiking, kayaking, and small-town daily walks. So he has learned through God's will and the sacred priesthood to love both country and city life!

Ordained now 29 years, he has recently enjoyed doing Religious Freedom Walks of 100 miles during summers from Hancock to Washington D.C., to Baltimore, and even in Ireland, France and this past summer in Italy. He also made a Pilgrimage of Love and Mercy, walking 100 miles from Baltimore to Philadelphia in honor of the papal visit of Pope Francis.

The great Lord has blessed him with marvelous health and he is very thankful for these many opportunities to serve as well as continue to learn the art and discipline of deeper prayer and meditation!

ADDITIONAL PRAISE

"This practical "Little Book" by Rev. Jack Lombardi is a profoundly simple, yet humble and helpful guide into a life of prayer, meditation and bible-focused spirituality. Commencing with a history of prayer, and providing entertaining anecdotes, vivid examples and helpful, down-to-earth steps on how-to meditate, this little book has reminded me, a prideful sinner, that the sure way to meet God in Christian meditation, is simply through practice. With the practical steps, and inspired wisdom of the author, I am once again motivated and prepared to continue to grow in my interior life through practice and perseverance. Thank you, Father Jack!"

− CATHERINE MILSTEAD
Founder, Christiana Homeschool Academy

CATHEDRAL FOUNDATION PRESS *a division of:*

CATHOLIC REVIEW MEDIA
Inform • Teach • Inspire • Engage

PARENT COMPANY OF:
The Catholic Review • Park Chase Press
Cathedral Foundation Press • Catholic Print Solutions

320 CATHEDRAL STREET • BALTIMORE, MD 21201 • 443-524-3150
PO BOX 777 • BALTIMORE, MD 21203 • CRMEDIA.ORG • CATHOLICREVIEW.ORG
PUBLISHED IN AMERICA'S PREMIER SEE − THE ARCHDIOCESE OF BALTIMORE